Barlow Cumberland

The Northern Lakes of Canada

With Sectional Maps of the Lakes and Illustrations

Barlow Cumberland

The Northern Lakes of Canada
With Sectional Maps of the Lakes and Illustrations

ISBN/EAN: 9783743442771

Manufactured in Europe, USA, Canada, Australia, Japa

Cover: Foto ©Andreas Hilbeck / pixelio.de

Manufactured and distributed by brebook publishing software (www.brebook.com)

Barlow Cumberland

The Northern Lakes of Canada

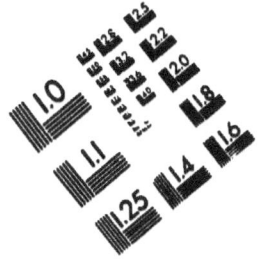 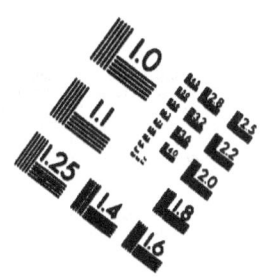

**IMAGE EVALUATION
TEST TARGET (MT-3)**

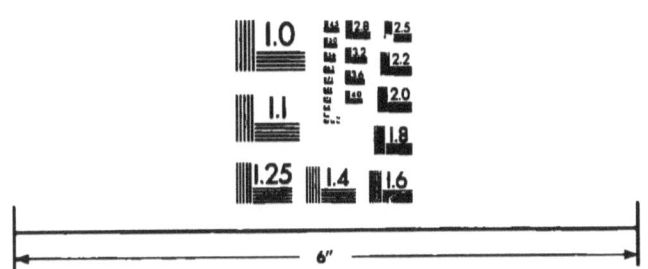

Photographic
Sciences
Corporation

23 WEST MAIN STREET
WEBSTER, N.Y. 14580
(716) 872-4503

Technical and Bibliographic Notes/Notes techniques et bibliographiques

The Institute has attempted to obtain the best original copy available for filming. Features of this copy which may be bibliographically unique, which may alter any of the images in the reproduction, or which may significantly change the usual method of filming, are checked below.

L'Institut a microfilmé le meilleur exemplaire qu'il lui a été possible de se procurer. Les détails de cet exemplaire qui sont peut-être uniques du point de vue bibliographique, qui peuvent modifier une image reproduite, ou qui peuvent exiger une modification dans la méthode normale de filmage sont indiqués ci-dessous.

☐ Coloured covers/
Couverture de couleur

☐ Covers damaged/
Couverture endommagée

☐ Covers restored and/or laminated/
Couverture restaurée et/ou pelliculée

☐ Cover title missing/
Le titre de couverture manque

☑ Coloured maps/
Cartes géographiques en couleur

☐ Coloured ink (i.e. other than blue or black)/
Encre de couleur (i.e. autre que bleue ou noire)

☐ Coloured plates and/or illustrations/
Planches et/ou illustrations en couleur

☐ Bound with other material/
Relié avec d'autres documents

☐ Tight binding may cause shadows or distortion along interior margin/
La reliure serrée peut causer de l'ombre ou de la distortion le long de la marge intérieure

☐ Blank leaves added during restoration may appear within the text. Whenever possible, these have been omitted from filming/
Il se peut que certaines pages blanches ajoutées lors d'une restauration apparaissent dans le texte, mais, lorsque cela était possible, ces pages n'ont pas été filmées.

☑ Additional comments:/
Commentaires supplémentaires: Various paging.

☑ Coloured pages/
Pages de couleur

☐ Pages damaged/
Pages endommagées

☑ Pages restored and/or laminated/
Pages restaurées et/ou pelliculées

☑ Pages discoloured, stained or foxed/
Pages décolorées, tachetées ou piquées

☐ Pages detached/
Pages détachées

☑ Showthrough/
Transparence

☐ Quality of print varies/
Qualité inégale de l'impression

☐ Includes supplementary material/
Comprend du matériel supplémentaire

☐ Only edition available/
Seule édition disponible

☐ Pages wholly or partially obscured by errata slips, tissues, etc., have been refilmed to ensure the best possible image/
Les pages totalement ou partiellement obscurcies par un feuillet d'errata, une pelure, etc., ont été filmées à nouveau de façon à obtenir la meilleure image possible.

The copy filmed here has been reproduced thanks
to the generosity of:

    Library of the Public
    Archives of Canada

The images appearing here are the best quality
possible considering the condition and legibility
of the original copy and in keeping with the
filming contract specifications.

Original copies in printed paper covers are filmed
beginning with the front cover and ending on
the last page with a printed or illustrated impression, or the back cover when appropriate. All
other original copies are filmed beginning on the
first page with a printed or illustrated impression, and ending on the last page with a printed
or illustrated impression.

The last recorded frame on each microfiche
shall contain the symbol —▶ (meaning "CONTINUED"), or the symbol ▼ (meaning "END"),
whichever applies.

Maps, plates, charts, etc., may be filmed at
different reduction ratios. Those too large to be
entirely included in one exposure are filmed
beginning in the upper left hand corner, left to
right and top to bottom, as many frames as
required. The following diagrams illustrate the
method:

L'exemplaire filmé fut reproduit grâce à la
générosité de:

    La bibliothèque des Archives
    publiques du Canada

Les images suivantes ont été reproduites avec le
plus grand soin, compte tenu de la condition et
de la netteté de l'exemplaire filmé, et en
conformité avec les conditions du contrat de
filmage.

Les exemplaires originaux dont la couverture en
papier est imprimée sont filmés en commençant
par le premier plat et en terminant soit par la
dernière page qui comporte une empreinte
d'impression ou d'illustration, soit par le second
plat, selon le cas. Tous les autres exemplaires
originaux sont filmés en commençant par la
première page qui comporte une empreinte
d'impression ou d'illustration et en terminant par
la dernière page qui comporte une telle
empreinte.

Un des symboles suivants apparaîtra sur la
dernière image de chaque microfiche, selon le
cas: le symbole —▶ signifie "A SUIVRE", le
symbole ▼ signifie "FIN".

Les cartes, planches, tableaux, etc., peuvent être
filmés à des taux de réduction différents.
Lorsque le document est trop grand pour être
reproduit en un seul cliché, il est filmé à partir
de l'angle supérieur gauche, de gauche à droite,
et de haut en bas, en prenant le nombre
d'images nécessaire. Les diagrammes suivants
illustrent la méthode.

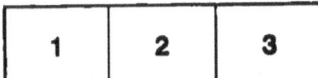

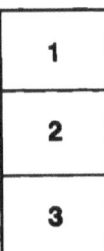

THE QUEEN'S HOTEL,
TORONTO.
STRICTLY FIRST-CLASS IN ALL ITS APPOINTMENTS.

Celebrated for its home comforts, perfect quiet, excellent attendance, and the peculiar excellence of its cuisine; it has been patronized by their Royal Highnesses Prince Leopold and the Princess Louise, the Marquis of Lorne, Lord and Lady Dufferin, the Marquis and Marchioness of Lansdowne, and the best families. Is most delightfully situated near the Bay, on Front Street, and is one of the largest and most comfortable hotels in the Dominion of Canada.

McGAW & WINNETT, Proprietors.

Queen's Royal Hotel,
NIAGARA-ON-THE-LAKE, ONT.

———o———

This Hotel and Summer Resort is located in a beautiful grove opposite Fort Niagara, at the head of Lake Ontario and the mouth of the Niagara River. It is capable of accommodating three hundred and fifty guests. All modern improvements. The drives along the banks of the Lake and River are beautiful and refreshing.

Application for rooms may be made to the proprietors of the Queen's Hotel, Toronto, up to June 1st, after that date to the "Queen's Royal," Niagara-on-the-Lake, Ont.

McGAW & WINNETT, Proprietors,

WALKER HOUSE,

TORONTO, ONTARIO, CANADA.

This favourite and commodious HOTEL is conveniently situated to the principal Railway Stations, Steamboat Landings, and the Parliament Buildings. It has ONE HUNDRED and TWENTY-FIVE WELL-VENTILATED BED-ROOMS besides spacious Public and Private Dining and Drawing Rooms. The house is heated throughout by steam, giving a comfortable temperature during the coldest weather; and its fine site, overlooking Toronto Bay on Lake Ontario, renders it a very desirable Summer resort.

TERMS :—$2.00 and $2.50 per day which includes room and attendance, with Full Board (Table d'Hote) from a Bill of Fare, comprising the best that the market affords.

The Transfer Hotel Omnibus and Luggage Waggon, and the "Walker House" Porter, attend to the arrivals of all Passenger Trains and Steamboats.

| HEAVY, SHELF AND GENERAL HARDWARE. | **RICE LEWIS & SON,** | IRON, STEEL WIRE, AND MANILLA ROPE. |

HARDWARE
—AND—
IRON MERCHANTS,
TORONTO.

Mechanics and Carpenters' Tools,
Builders', Foundry and Boat Supplies,
Table and Pocket Cutlery,
Plated Forks and Spoons,
PATENT THREE ROLLER MANGLES,
A FULL and WELL ASSORTED STOCK OF HARDWARE.

W. A. BRADSHAW,

23 East Market Square, Toronto,

GROCER AND SHIP CHANDLER,

ANCHORS,	CHAINS,
ROPE,	BLOCKS,
OAKUM,	PAINTS and OILS.

Camping Parties' Outfits.

SOLICITED ORDERS PROMPTLY ATTENDED TO.

JOHN MALLON & CO.,

Nos. 12 to 16 ST. LAWRENCE MARKET,

TORONTO.

FAMILY BUTCHERS,

HAVE ALWAYS ON HAND

MESS BEEF—CHOICEST BRANDS,

IN CAR LOTS OR SMALLER QUANTITIES.

VERRAL'S
Cab, Coupe, Livery & Boarding Stables.

ESTABLISHED 1855.

HEAD OFFICE & STABLES,—11, 13, 15, 17 & 19 Mercer St.
Telephone No., 979.
BRANCH,—11 & 13 Queen St. East.
Telephone No., 938.

Visitors and Tourists will study their own interest by sending all orders to us, and insure good turnouts at Tariff Rates.

Excursionists can order cabs by telephone from the "Chicora" Office.

HIGHEST REFERENCE.   OFFICES NEVER CLOSED.

GEO. VERRAL,
Proprietor.

D. PIKE,
MANUFACTURER OF
TENTS, AWNINGS, FLAGS,

Horse and Waggon Covers, Life Preservers,

Waterproof Bags, Lawn and Canvas Hammocks.

TENTS TO RENT,
AND DIFFERENT GRADES OF CANVAS ALWAYS ON HAND.

Special attention given to the requirements of Hunting and Fishing Camping Parties. Tents for Sportsmen, or Compartment Tents for Families. All correspondence by mail promptly answered and Price Lists forwarded on application.

D. PIKE, 157 King St. East, Toronto, Ont.

MILLMAN & CO.,
(Late **NOTMAN & FRASER**.)

PHOTOGRAPHIC ARTISTS,

41 KING STREET EAST,

TORONTO.

MESSRS. MILLMAN & Co., have refitted the Studio throughout, and adopted all the newest improvements, making it the finest Photographic establishment in Canada, and although doing a superior class of work, their prices are low. All the negatives of the late firm have been preserved.

W. McDOWALL,
—IMPORTER OF—
Fine Guns, Fishing Tackle, Camping Goods, &c.

Just received a splendid assortment of Rods and Tackle; also a complete line of Base Ball supplies. Guns and tents rented. Price list free.

W. McDOWALL, 67 KING ST. EAST, TORONTO.

OCEAN HOUSE,
BURLINGTON BEACH, ONTARIO.

Bathing, Boating, and Fishing. No mosquitoes. *Every room in this House fronts on the water.*

THE LONG BRANCH OF CANADA.
CAMPBELL & HILL, · · · · · · · **PROPRIETORS.**

TORONTO, HAMILTON AND OAKVILLE.
STEAMER
"SOUTHERN BELLE,"
—AND—
Grand Trunk Railway.

Leave by boat and return by any train, or leave by train and return by boat.

Toronto to Hamilton and return, or *vice versa*, good one day, $1.25; good three days, $1.60; Saturday excursion good by boat Saturday to return by train on Monday a.m., $1.00; single fare by steamer, 75c.

Steamer will leave Mowat's Wharf daily (weather permitting) at 11 o'clock a.m., and 5.30 p.m. For departure and arrival of trains see G. T. R. time-table. Season trip tickets and bi-weekly excursions.

WM. EDGAR, *G.T.R.*   **A. & G. KEITH,** *Str. "Southern Belle."*

WATCHES.   DIAMONDS.
ESTABLISHED 1830.
JAMES E. ELLIS & CO.
BY APPOINTMENT

Official, Government, Railway and City Timekeepers,

IMPORTERS AND MANUFACTURERS OF

FINE GOLD WATCHES, JEWELLERY,

Sterling Silver and Plated Ware, Diamonds, French Clocks and Bronzes, Split Seconds and Repeating Watches.

LARGEST STOCK IN THE PROVINCE. LOWEST PRICES.

ALL GOODS GUARANTEED.

JAMES E. ELLIS & CO.,
No. 1 KING STREET EAST, TORONTO.

THE LEHIGH VALLEY RAILROAD.

Double Track, Steel Rails, Elegantly Equipped.

Affords you the finest view of

Beautiful Scenery
EAST OF THE ROCKIES.

Through the Famous Switzerland of America, Mauch Chunk, Glen Onoko, and the beautiful Wyoming Valley.

ELEGANT DAY EXPRESS.

Solid Eastlake Train between New York or Philadelphia and Buffalo, Suspension Bridge or Niagara Falls (daily except Sunday).   Night Express (Daily) between the same points.

CITY TICKET OFFICES :—

NEW YORK—235 Broadway.   -   PHILADELPHIA—836 Chestnut Street.
BUFFALO—Cor. Main and Seneca Streets.

Mauch Chunk, Pa.   E. B. BYINGTON, Genl. Pass. Agt.

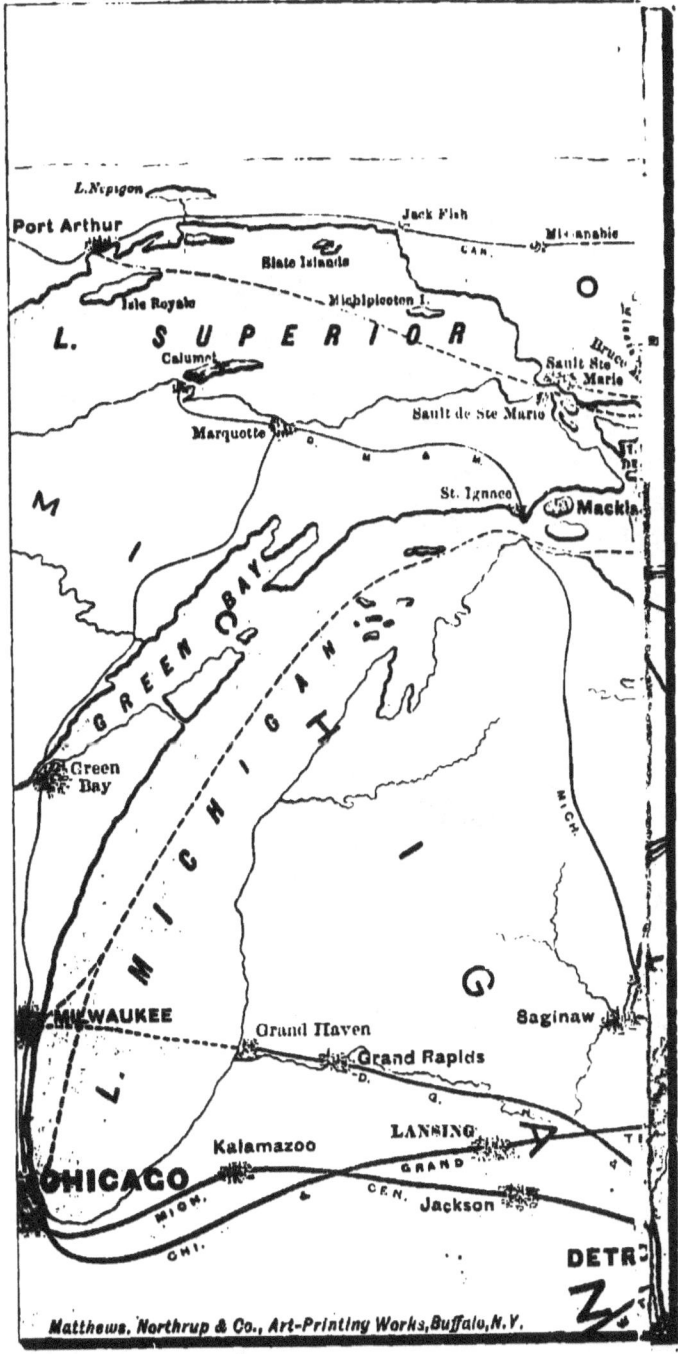

Matthews, Northrup & Co., Art-Printing Works, Buffalo, N.Y.

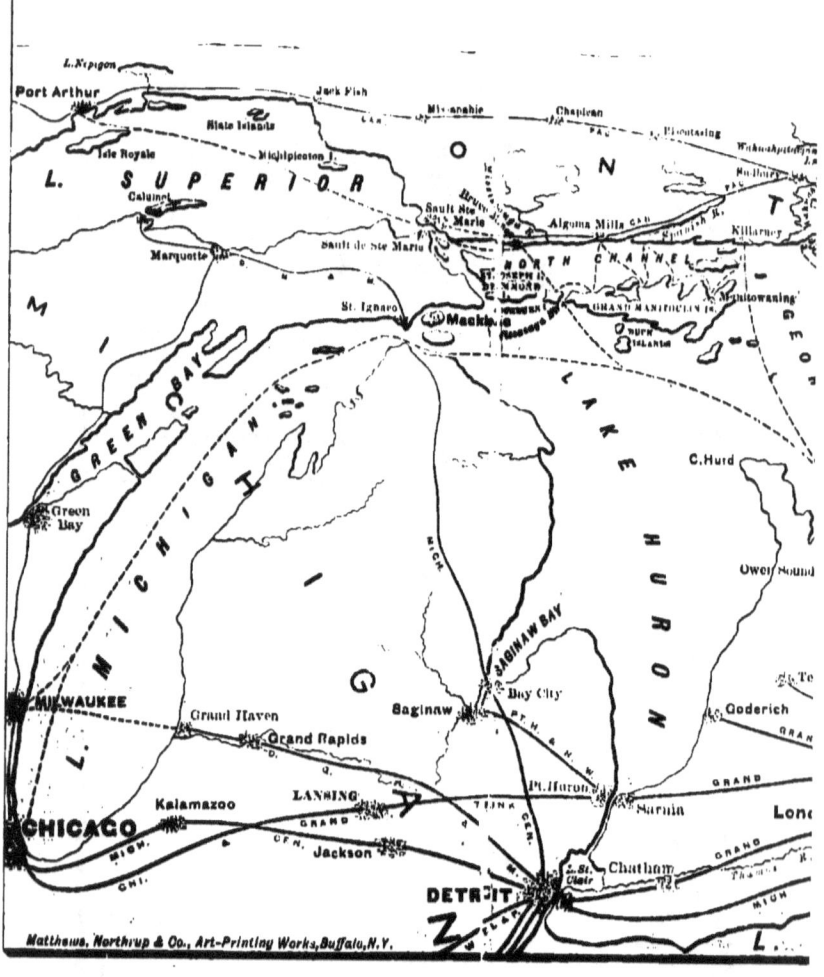

Lakes

a.

AND COUCHICHING,

Muskoka,

ITOULIN CHANNEL,
LAKE SUPERIOR.

S—HOTELS—CAMPING
NG —DISTANCES
EL.

AND ILLUSTRATIONS.

...LAND.

TORONTO.

Toronto:
HUNTER, ROSE & CO., PRINTERS.

1886

Northern Lakes

OF

Canada.

THE NIAGARA RIVER AND TORONTO,
LAKES SIMCOE AND COUCHICHING,

The Lakes of Muskoka,

THE GEORGIAN BAY, GREAT MANITOULIN CHANNEL,
MACKINAC, SAULT STE. MARIE, LAKE SUPERIOR.

A GUIDE TO THE

BEST SPOTS FOR WATERSIDE RESORTS—HOTELS—CAMPING
OUTFIT, FISHING AND SHOOTING—DISTANCES
AND COST OF TRAVEL.

WITH

SECTIONAL MAPS OF THE LAKES AND ILLUSTRATIONS.

EDITED BY
BARLOW CUMBERLAND,
TORONTO.

Toronto:
HUNTER, ROSE & CO., PRINTERS.

1886

With compliments of

Barlow Cumberland

Entered according to Act of Parliament of Canada, in the year one thousand eight hundred and eighty-six, by BARLOW CUMBERLAND, in the office of the Minister of Agriculture.

PAAP
FC
3067.3
C84

THE
NORTHERN LAKES
OF CANADA.

A Little Farther On.

It may fairly be said that there is scarcely a tourist who lands on the shores of America, who does not visit NIAGARA FALLS, and there are thousands of inhabitants of this Continent who feel impelled to follow their example.

Not to have seen Niagara in these days of rapid communication, is to admit one's self to be behind the age, therefore, it is, that as in Europe, the old saying is, "All the roads lead to Rome," so on this continent all the routes lead to Niagara Falls, and everybody can go there if they will.

The object of this little sketch may frankly be avowed to be that when the visitor shall have reached Niagara, it may, by telling him truthfully what there is beyond, encourage him to come a *little farther on*.

It may be he will come only to the mouth of the NIAGARA RIVER and back. (See page 15). Here he will visit the most historic scenes in this land, where every height tells some thrilling tale of martial valour, of victory, or of death, and each succeeding turn of the winding River opens out a vista of recollection or landscape beauty, whose present peace makes pleasant the tale of past and stirring war.

Or, should he come from some inland country, where ponds are called lakes, and little streamlets gurgle as rivers with high-sounding names, let us tempt him to cross a Lake as large as many a salty sea, and voyaging in an ocean-going steamer, for a short time *lose sight of land*, upon a fresh water trip to the most busy and thriving city in Canada. It is of itself a little episode, this rapid trip across the Lake Ontario.

In TORONTO, he will find a change of scene combining the push and smart energy of the Yankee, with the solid and phlegmatic surety of the Briton. A city of churches and fine public buildings, of healthful moral tendencies, and broad streets studded with many happy homes. The centre of the mental culture of the land, with Public Libraries for the enquiring, Universities and Colleges for the learned, and Parks and Island waterside resorts for the athletically inclined.

For many years the visitor to Canada has swept along the border, taking the "Rapid" trip down the mighty St. Lawrence to the sea. Let him be tempted to stay a while, and go a *little farther on* into the interior of the country, to the "NORTHERN LAKES OF CANADA," where primeval forests jostle close with summer hotels, and nature can be studied and enjoyed, freed from the artificialities of every-day city life.

They are not places to which to go, for display of fine clothes or many changes of raiment, to see dusty crowds hurry past in herds, measuring their pleasures by the mileage over which they rush, but *they are* places where within convenient and cheap distance of the

LANDING A MASKINONGE.

great highways, exist high altitude and pure air, pretty scenes and mingled land and waterscape; where game laws are respected and fishing carefully preserved, as being the greatest source of attraction to the work-worn city man; where rest from the busy whirl can most surely be obtained; and whether it be under the canvas covering of the camp, or in the comfortable bed of an unpretentious hotel, the resin-laden smell of the sighing pine and soft lappings of the little wavelets on the quiet shores will lull the weary brain to sound and unaccustomed sleep.

The District of the LAKES OF MUSKOKA, is a region of many, many lakes of all sizes and forms, where canoeing and boating from hamlet to hamlet along the shores, combines the safety of a scattered population with the wildness of uncultivated wastes. This is no matter of choice or taste with the hardy settler, for nature has so accumulated the rocks and wilds along the shores that only at intervening spots can sufficient breadth of soil be found on which to farm. The Hotels are not great caravansaries, but moderate houses where plain meals, fresh milk, cleanly rooms and *comfortable* as distinguished from *elegant* accompaniments, are joined with *moderate* as distinguished from *high priced* charges. This does not mean " Roughing it in the Bush," but that the common simple wants are fully supplied, and the extra velvets and sauces of city civilization are left at home. A glance at the details hereinafter shown will tell at how little cost a whole family can have a happy holiday for what indeed in other directions would little more than pay their railway fares.

But should our tourist wish to stray still *a little farther on* and spend his time in steamers on the Lakes, we will take him for day after day upon the great upper water through the beauties of GEORGIAN BAY, with its channels winding to the north of the *Great Manitoulin Island*, in sheltered courses, but with unsullied winds fresh from their far off homes in the now nearing North, so shall he reach Sault Ste. Marie, or *Mackinac* and its many diverging routes, or sailing out upon the broad expanse of the mighty LAKE SUPERIOR, the largest lake in all the world, visit the lofty shores of *Thunder Bay*, *Port Arthur* and *Duluth*, the "city of the unsalted seas."

Study, reader, these few leaves and learning that Canada is not simply a strip along the coast, make up your mind to breathe a little of the air beneath the Red Cross flag, and entering upon the border venture yet—*a little farther on*.

For the East and South.

It has been already said that from all points of America Rates and Routes can be obtained to and from Niagara Falls, but there are some railways which are preeminent in the numbers they transport and in the territory they embrace, and as it may be useful to passengers taking the Niagara River Route from Toronto, some of these may be mentioned.

THE HUDSON RIVER ROUTE.

Having crossed the lake by the Niagara Navigation Company's steamer Chicora, direct connection is made at *Lewiston* with the *New York Central Railway*. Baggage is examined on board and checked to destination for holders of through tickets. Once upon the express trains of the New York Central Railway, progress to the Atlantic shore is swift and certain. The *only four track* railway in America, two of its lines are given up entirely to passenger trains; the other two being occupied only by freight trains; there are therefore no trains to meet and no trains to pass, but a regular flow of traffic moves uninterruptedly in one direction along each track. No wonder, therefore, the wheels seem to ring along with unvarying regularity like the steady beating of an unruffled heart. Keeping about the course of the Erie Canal, through the level plains and salt pastures of the Onondaga District, the picturesque *Mohawk Valley* is next followed from its rising waters, near Rome, to its junction with the Hudson, near Albany. Thence the rails just above the level of the river's surface follow the left banks of the noble *Hudson*, with all its varied river craft and glorious scenery, passing through the "*Gateways of the Catskills*" and in front of the *Palisades* of its lower reaches, to the great city, New York.

At *Lewiston* connection is made also with the *West Shore Railway* —the latest addition to the great Trunk lines—under the same management and direction as the New York Central; it forms another link through much the same line of country to Albany. From here it follows down the opposite side of the river, skirting the west or right bank of the great *Hudson*, and sweeping along under the very foot of the lofty mountains until at length, when near the lower end, it leaves the river and curving into the midst of the valleys, makes a short detour from the banks to return again opposite New York, to whose streets the passenger is conveyed by ferry. With new and splendid equipment and the most modern and instructed track alignment, its claims on the traveller's patronage combine novelty with perfect performance.

Should passengers holding the Niagara Navigation Company's tickets to New York, by either of these Railways, so desire they can break their journey at Albany and go down the river by the palatial steamers of the *Day Line*.

The Eastern shores of Massachusets and Boston are reached by train from Albany.

THE DELAWARE VALLEY ROUTE.

At Niagara-on-the-Lake the steamer makes direct connection with the Michigan Central Railway, whose trains run alongside on the dock. By these, at *Suspension Bridge*, on the Canadian side, junction is made with the Express trains of the far-famed *Erie R. R.* Having crossed "the Bridge" the trains follow the shore to *Buffalo*; from here begins the scenery which has created the name and renown of "Picturesque Erie." At *Portage*, from the lofty bridge

THE STARUCCA VIADUCT.

which spans the cleft, a complete view is gained of the dizzy cliffs three hundred feet sheer in height, and of the Genesee River, winding far away below. Farther on are the valleys of the *Chenango* and

Susquehanna Rivers, with rifts and mountain crags, and rushing streams, where views abound which artists have come from afar to reproduce, and the massive arches of the *Starucca Viaduct* act as a foil to the surrounding scene.

Over the heights and nearer the Atlantic shore, the fair vales of the *Delaware* bring the swift train to Jersey City and New York. The Erie is celebrated for the excellence of its cars and completness of its equipments which are unsurpassed by any. Direct connections are made by it with the Lehigh Valley R. R. for Philadelphia and Washington by a route proverbial for its beauty.

Travellers to or from the South shores of Lake Erie on the *Lake Shore and Michigan Southern R. R.*, or on any railway system passing through Buffalo, can obtain at all principal Railway stations, tickets via the *Niagara River* to Toronto.

To and From the West.

OF the great highways between Chicago, Detroit, Niagara Falls and Buffalo, there is none that has sprung more quickly into life, vigour and the appreciation of the travelling public than the Michigan Central Railway. An air line from lake to lake, with only one curve in each hundred miles; a track made and laid as good as good can be; cars of the finest and engines of the swiftest, it has earned a record for speed, successful punctuality and safety, that brings grist to its mill, increasing every day that it runs. It was a *big bang* when, in May, '81, Cornelius Vanderbilt swept over the road two hundred and twenty-nine miles in two hundred and thirty-five minutes, but they " Outbanged Bannager " when the " Parsons," on their special train, made one hundred and eleven miles in one hundred and nine minutes, beating the " Commodore's " time by three minutes over the same part of the road! As we are not all Railway Magnates or Angels in disguise, it isn't to be supposed that we, too, shall fly along at this rate, but instances such as these prove the character of the road, and account for the unwarying reliability with which it does its duty to its patrons.

But the *Picturesque* is not forgotten in the *Practical*, and the managers have not failed to avail themselves of the unexampled natural advantages which the location of the railway presents.

MICHIGAN CENTRAL TRAIN PASSING FALLS VIEW STATION.

At *Falls View* the rail follows the brink of the Niagara River just where the waters begin to hurry to the brink of the cataract. And here, on the lofty bank, a station platform has been placed, at which all trains stop, giving passengers ten minutes in which to alight and enjoy the view of the falls.

The whole panorama lies at one glance before the eye, and the onlooker almost shrinks back from the stout railing of the platform as, watching the eddying waves, he peers over the edge of the seething gulf into which they are relentlessly thrown.

THE NORTHERN LAKES OF CANADA.   11

The most hurried traveller, whose time does not permit his stopping over to pay a visit in detail to Niagara, may feel assured that in these few minutes which the Michigan Central Company give him in his way between the east and the west, he has indeed seen the Falls.

A PEEP AT THE AMERICAN FALL.

Niagara Falls.

It is not within the scope of this little guide to give enlarged mention of the beauties and scenery about Niagara Falls, such information being better obtained from the local guide-books; but a few notes may be useful to visitors.

But a short time since Niagara Falls had gained an unenviable notoriety for the expenses—if not indeed to be termed extortions—which obliged every visitor to pay for the privilege of obtaining access to any point from which the Falls could be viewed.

Particularly was this the case on the American side, but now all has been changed, and "Free Niagara" calls all the world to come and view its beauties, now restored to their primitive condition, as the greatest wonder of Nature on the Continent.

In 1885 the State of New York appropriated $1,433,000 to the purchase of the lands surrounding the cataract; the Province of Ontario is engaged in the same work on the Canadian side.

To see the falls thoroughly used to cost for admissions over $5; but now the whole is thrown open *free*, excepting, of course, such extras as passing under the Falls or crossing the ferry, or over the Suspension Bridge. A visitor can conveniently visit the whole on foot, or take the line of street cars which run between the Whirlpool and the Cataract. There are thousands who have been at "the Falls," yet have never seen the Falls; a re-visit will now be in order, and more happiness be obtained than was possible when every step had to be paid for, and every peep cost a sigh.

Visitors from Toronto can leave in the morning by steamer and after spending five hours at the falls, can return and arrive home again early the same evening.

There is such a magnitude of interest, such a constant variety of wonders, that neither mind nor eye becomes satiated with watching the wondrous cataract or its surrounding scenes.

With such facilities for travel, it is better to take several visits and study each portion in detail.

The little map which here appears, gives a list of all the places which should be visited, and aided by it, the visitor can easily find his way about.

Passengers *via Niagara* take the *Michigan Central R.R.* (late C.S.R.) The depot is near the Clifton House, on the Canadian side. Passengers *via Lewiston*, on the American side, take *New York Central R.R.* The depot is marked " 8 " on the plan.

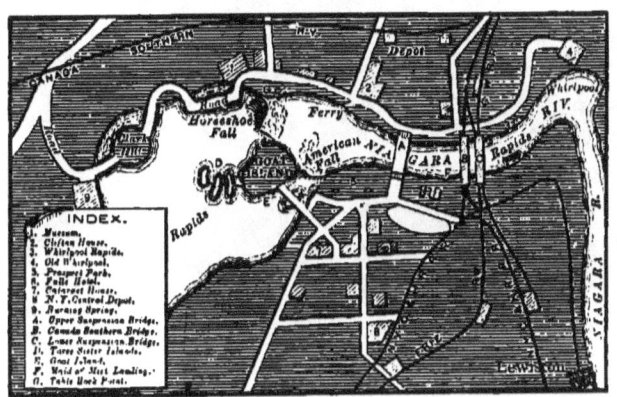

POINTS OF INTEREST AT THE FALLS.

The expense of visiting Niagara Falls, other than the amount paid for travelling, depends entirely upon the habits or fancy of the visitor. The cost of seeing the place is now *nothing*. A tariff has been arranged for cabs, and good bargains can often be made by those who wish to drive.

There are numerous restaurants where good meals can be obtained at reasonable rates, and hotels exist of every variety, from $1 to $4 per day. No doubt the old pastime of *staying* at the Falls, instead of *hurrying away* from them, will once more return, now that the expenses of *seeing* the place can be applied to paying the hotel bill, or, perhaps, in purchasing some memento of the visit. In this latter respect, don't fail to see " Libbie and Katie."

ON THE CANADIAN SIDE.

On the Canadian side, upon the edge of the new park and on the verge of the cliff with its spacious verandahs facing the American Falls, stands the *Clifton House*. The pillars of the verandahs may be noted as being formed each from the single trunk ot so many giant pines. In earlier days whole part of these magnificent trees covered the adjacent shores and on not a few of the porticos of the more important residences will similar use be seen to have been made of their convenient form.

THE CLIFTON HOUSE.

PRINCIPAL HOTELS AT NIAGARA FALLS.

Cataract House	American side		Capacity	750
International Hotel..	"		"	625
Spencer House	"		"	175
Niagara House	"		"	100
Pacific Hotel	"		"	80
Goat Island Hotel	"		"	60
Hotel Kaltenbach	"		"	60
Rapids House	"		"	40
Temperance House	"		"	40
Clifton House	Canadian side		"	250
Prospect House	"		"	100
Brunswick House	"		"	100
Robinson House	"		"	40

The Niagara River.
Between the Falls and Lake Ontario.

There are two routes by which the visitor can travel between Buffalo, Niagara Falls and Toronto. The one on the American side of the River, by the *New York Central R. R.*, to Lewiston, the other on the Canadian side, (see page 27), by the *Michigan Central R. R.*, to Niagara-on-the-Lake.

ALONG THE AMERICAN SIDE.

MAP NIAGARA RIVER.

The New York Central skirts the shores of the River on the American side, and just after passing the Suspension Bridge Station curves sharply round and leaving the level open land dips into and runs along a shelf or ledge which has been boldly cut out from the face of the mighty cleft through which the River runs downwards to the lake. On the one side the cars hug close to the towering cliff, on the other, far down below, over the debris and the blocks of tossed and shattered rocks the waters are seen swirling along in the tumultuous foamings of the WHIRLPOOL RAPIDS. The train is in the very gorge itself; a glimpse is caught of the sullen solemn whirlpool where the mighty flood arrested for a time in its downward rush slowly circles around, chafing and grinding against the confining barriers; suddenly it reaches the long sought for outlet and springing anew into re-invigoured life, dashes the beads of foam from its exultant waves high into the air, and gleefully resumes its onward rapid course. Now slipping through tunnels under the projecting cliffs, now sweeping in curves around the jutting headlands and giving distant vistas up and down the stream and of the glorious view over the borderland towards the lake, the train gradually approaches the waters' surface; the broken remains of the Queenstown Suspension Bridge come into view, and high above, the monument to Brock.

LEWISTON, the head of navigation, is seven miles from the Falls, and the visitor walks from the railway to the deck of the Niagara Company's steamer waiting for him at the dock.

Great care is always taken along this portion of the railway, and,

THE NEW YORK CENTRAL IN THE GORGE.

never has any accident occurred. The steamer turns in the eddy of he rapids which close just a little above the dock. On the opposite shore is Queenston and the scene of the battle of Queenston Heights. The first point below the town is Vrooman's Point, and now for another seven miles the river winds in many curves between high and wooded banks, along the edge of which are seen comfortable mansions set in the midst of the peach orchards, which have made the district a very fruit garden; three miles from the mouth is *Three mile run* where the Canadians crossed to attack Fort Niagara, and at the mouth itself are the American village of Youngstown, and on the opposite shore Niagara-on-the Lake. Beyond them are seen the blue waters of Lake Ontario.

The "Gorge" of Niagara.

By the Duke of Argyll.

" A very curious question, and one of great scientific interest arises out of the great difference between the course of the Niagara River above and below the Falls. It has in my opinion, been much too readily assumed by geologists that rivers have excavated the valleys in which they run. The cutting power of water is very great, but it varies in proportion to the liability of floods, and the wearing power of stones that may be carried along: much also depends on the position of the rocks over which a river runs. If the stratification present edges which are easily attacked or undermined, even a gentle stream may cut rapidly for itself a deeper bed. On the other hand when the rocks do not expose any surfaces which are easily assailable a very large body of water may run over them for ages without being able to scoop out more than a few feet or even a few inches.

Accordingly such is actually the case with the Niagara River in the upper part of its course from Lake Erie to the Falls. In all the ages during which it has run in that course for fifteen miles it has not been able to remove more than a few feet of soil or rock. The country is level, and the banks are very low, so low that in looking up the bed of the stream the more distant trees on either bank seem to rise out of the water.

THE PRECIPICE AT THE HORSE-SHOE FALLS.

But suddenly in the middle of the comparatively level country the river encounters a precipice, and thence forward for seven miles runs through a profound cleft or ravine the bottom of which is not less than 300 feet below the general level of the country.

How came that precipice to be there? This would be no puzzle at all if the precipice were joined with a sudden change in the general level of the country on either side of the river—and there is such a change—but it is not at the Falls. It is seven miles further on.

At the Falls there is no depression in the general level of the banks. Indeed, on the Canadian shore, the land rises very considerably just above the Falls. On the American shore it continues at the same elevation. The whole country here, however, is a table-land, and that table-land has a termination—an edge—over which the river must fall before it can reach Lake Ontario.

But that edge does not run across the country at Niagara Falls, but along a line much nearer to Lake Ontario, where it is a conspicuous feature in the landscape, and is called *Queenston Heights*.

The natural place, therefore, so to speak, for the Falls would have been where the river came to that edge, and from that point the river has all the appearance of having cut its way backward in the course of time.

Sir Charles Lyell, the eminent geologist, came to the conclusion, from comparison of the rate at which the cutting back had been observable within the memory of man, that this cutting back is about one foot in each year. At this rate the river would have taken 35,000 years to effect its retreat from Queenston to the present position of the Falls.

This is but a very short fathom-line to throw out into the abysmal depths of geological time, and making every allowance for the possibility of any differences in rate, according to variations of temperature or configuration, the principle of the calculation seems to be a sound one.

The strata or layers of rock which compose the geological formation can readily be seen in the gorge of the river, and the process by which the cataract has eaten its way back from Queenston can be readily perceived. At the level of the brink of the Falls, where the waters make their final plunge, are thick, regular and flat layers of limestone rock. Above and below these is soft soluble shale. The running water wearing away the upper deposits makes the inequalities which cause the rapids above the Falls, and the reverberation and splash of the torrent as it falls, have disintegrated and washed out the

THE "LEDGE" FROM THE AMERICAN SIDE.

soft red shale below, so that the limestone ledge is left in overhanging masses until they break off with their own weight, and piece after piece dropping into the depths beneath, the Falls continue their ceaseless march commenced so many centuries ago.

This deep groove does seem to be a clear case of a ravine produced by a known cause which can be seen now in actual operation. As far as I could see, there is nothing to indicate that the ravine is due to a " fault " or a crack arising from subterranean disturbance, but the work has been done by the process which has been described, and 35,000 years is, after all, but an insignificant fraction of what has been occupied in the operations of geological time."

Queenston Heights—where the Falls once were.

If the Cataract of Niagara had continued to be where it once was, it would have given additional splendour to one of the most beautiful landscapes of the world. Instead of falling, as it now does, into a narrow chasm, where it cannot be seen a few yards from either bank, it would have poured its magnificent torrent over a higher range of cliff, and would have shone for hundreds of miles over land and sea. The steep line of heights above Queenston form the termination or escarpement of the comparatively high table-land of the upper Lakes. On the summit of the ridge has been erected

BROCK'S MONUMENT.

This magnificent structure was erected by his grateful countrymen, to the memory of the brave General, who gallantly fell in the action which took place here on the 13th of October, 1812. The spot near a thorn bush, where he received his death wound, is further down the side of the hill, and marked by a monumental stone. The remains of the General, which had been interred in Fort George, at Niagara, together with those of his faithful *aide camp*, Lt-Col. John

McDonell, were in 1824 removed and placed beneath the first monument at that time erected. This having in 1840 been seriously damaged with explosives by a vandal named Lett, public sentiment was aroused and by a spontaneous movement, the necessary sum was immediately raised for the present unique structure.

The previous monument was erected by a grant from the Parliament of the Province, this one, from the voluntary contributions of the Militia and Indian warriors of the country.

On the 13th of October, 1853, the remains of the revered dead were again removed, to be placed where they now lie in massive stone sarcophogi beneath the column.

To gather some idea of the fervour which has raised so distinguished a memorial, we may quote from the speeches made on the spot, where twenty-eight years after his death it was determined that this second memorial should be raised. Speaking to the assembly some 8,000 in number, which had come enthusiastically from all parts of the province, *Mr. Justice Macaulay*, who had served under Brock, said, " Looking at the animated mass covering these sacred heights in 1840, to do honour for a war in 1812, now old in history, one is prompted to ask, ' How comes it that the gallant General has left so lasting an impression in the hearts of his countrymen, how comes it that the fame of Brock thus floats down the stream of time, broad, deep and fresh as the waters of the famed river with whose waves it might be almost said his life's blood mingled? In reply, we might dwell on his civil and military virtues, his patriotic self-devotion, his chivalrous gallantry and his triumphant achievements.

Still, there was more that gave him talismanic influence and ascendancy over his fellow men, and which he wielded for his country's good. His was the mind instinctively to conceive and promptly to dare—incredible things to feeble hearts. With skill and bearing he infused his chivalrous and enterprising spirit into all his followers and impelled them to realize whatever he boldly led the way to accomplish."

Sir John Beverley Robinson, then the venerable Chief Justice, but who, as a young man had fought with distinction alongside the deceased General, on the fatal, yet, glorious day, so long before, gave his testimony.

"It has been sometimes objected, that General Brock's courage was greater than his prudence, that his attack on Detroit, though it succeeded, was most likely to have failed, and that a similar rashness was displayed in the manner of his death. Those who lived here while these events were passing, can form a truer judgment; they know that what to some may seem rashness, was, in fact prudence, unless, indeed the defence of Canada was to be abandoned in the almost desperate circumstances in which, General Brock was placed. He had with him but a handful of men who had never been used to military discipline, few indeed who had seen actual service, and he knew it must be some time before any reinforcement could be sent him. He felt, therefore, his cause was hopeless, unless he could impress this truth upon the enemy, that whenever a General with but a few gallant soldiers, and the brave defenders of the soil could be assembled against them, they must retire from the land which they had invaded. If he had begun to compare numbers and had reserved his small force, in order to make a safer effort on a future day, then would thousands of the people from the neighbouring States have been found pouring into this Province. True, he fell in discharging a duty which might have been committed to a subordinate hand. True, he might have reserved himself for a more deliberate and stronger effort; but he felt that hesitation might be ruin, that all depended upon his dauntless courage and self-devotion. It is true his gallant course was arrested by a fatal wound, such is the fortune of war, but the people of Canada did not feel that his precious life was therefore thrown away, deeply as they deplored his fall.

His was an inflexible integrity, an honesty of character, uncommon energy and decision, and above all, an entire devotion to his country. In short, I believe I shall best convey an impression of him, when I say that it would have required more courage to refuse to follow General Brock, than to go with him wherever he would lead."

From these we can learn the estimate in which he was held. Long may this memorial remain to record the gallant deeds, and remind the youth of Canada ever to be ready to emulate his and their Fathers' valour in gallant defence of their happy native land.

The Monument

is of massive stone, in the base, entered by an oaken door, are two galleries on the north and south sides of which are the tombs of the illustrious dead. From the ground to the gallery at the top is a circular staircase of cut stone with 235 steps, and the magnificent view of the surrounding country is obtained through the circular wreathed openings. From the exterior the column is of the Roman composite order, with a sculptured capital containing figures of victory holding military shields. On the summit is a collossal statue of the Hero in military uniform, the left hand resting on the sword, the right hand extended with baton.

The height from the ground is 190 feet, exceeding that of any other monumental column, either ancient or modern, with the single exception of that of the Great Fire of London, which exceeds it by only twelve feet.

On the exterior of the base are lions rampant, and on the side facing Queenston, the battle scene, in alto relievo.

The grounds are well laid out, and on the gates are the arms of the Brock family.

The caretaker's lodge is close by, and a small fee is charg'd for admission.

Comparative heights of some principal monuments of the same kind, ancient and modern.

	FT.
Trajans pillar, Rome	115.0
Antonine column, Rome	123.
Duke of York's column, London	137.
Monument of Great Fire, London	202.
Napoleon column, Paris	132.
Vendome column, Paris	156.
Alexander column, St. Petersburgh	176.6
Nelson's column, Trafalgar Square, London	171.

THE VIEW FROM THE SUMMIT.

Having clambered to the summit of the heights, and ascended to the top of the monument, a scene is met with, than which, few others

BROCK'S MONUMENT AND THE MOUTH OF THE NIAGARA.
[QUEENSTON]
[LEWISTON]

in America leave such an impression on the mind. It is altogether peculiar, unlike anything in the Old World, and such as few spots can command in the New.

One great glory of the American continent is its Lakes and rivers. But they are generally too large to make much impression on the eye. The rivers are often so broad as to look like lakes without their picturesqueness, and the lakes are so large as to look like the Sea, but without so great grandeur. Another great glory of America, is its vast breadths of habitable surface. But these again, are also so vast that there are few spots indeed, whence they can be seen and estimated. But from the heights of Queenston, both these great features are spread out before the eye after a manner in which they can be taken in. The steep bank below is covered with *thaja occidentalis* commonly called the cedar. Looking to the north-east, the horizon is occupied by the blue waters of Lake Ontario, which form the sky-line. But on either hand, the shores can be seen bending round the Lake to an illimitable distance, and losing themselves in fading tints of blue. To the left, turning towards the north-west, the fair Province of Ontario stretches in immense plains and escarpements of the same table-land.

The whole of this immense extent of country has the aspect of a land comfortably settled, widely cultivated and beautifully clothed with trees. Towns and villages are indicated by little spots of gleaming white, by smoke, and a few church spires.

On the Canadian shore, and forty miles away over the deep Lake, the City of Toronto is sometimes distinctly visible, when the atmosphere is clear, the elevation of the height overcoming the intervening distance. At our feet the magnificent river of the Niagara emerges from its ravine, into the open sunlight of the plains, and winds slowly in long reaches of lonely green, and round a succession of low-wooded capes into the vast waters of Ontario. The contrast is very striking between the perfect restfulness of the current here, and the tormented violence of its course at the Falls, and the Rapids.

The wide landscape seen from Brock's monument along the shores of Lake Ontario, on both sides of the river as far as the eye can reach, exhibits throughout the same characteristic features.

THE
CANADIAN PACIFIC
RAILWAY

Is THE TRUE

Transcontinental Route.

Is THE TRUE

Sportsman's Route.

Is THE TRUE

Tourist's Route.

Is THE TRUE

Invalid's Route.

Is THE TRUE

Scenic Route.

☞ *Send for a Guide of this truly wonderful line.*
W. R. CALLAWAY, Dist. Pass. Agt, 110 King St. West, TORONTO, ONT.
W. C. VAN HORNE,   GEO. OLDS,   D. McNICOLL,
   Vice-President. Gen'l Traffic Manager.   Gen'l Pass. Agent.
                  MONTREAL.

THE ONLY STEAMERS ON
INSIDE ROUTE
TO
PARRY SOUND

PARRY SOUND NAVIGATION CO.
STEAMERS "MAXWELL" AND "CHICOUTIMI,"
Connecting with Northern and North-Western Railroad.
Leave Midland and Penetang on arrival of morning trains from Toronto.
Returning, Leave Parry Sound 6 a.m. daily, except Sunday.

THROUGH ALL THE ISLANDS BY DAYLIGHT.
For Rates and Tickets apply to all Agents N. & N.-W. R. R., and

Barlow Cumberland,   John Pearse,
35 Yonge Street, Toronto.   Manager, Parry Harbor.

PENETANGUISHENE.
GEORGIAN BAY HOUSE.
This New Hotel favourably situated, facing the waters of the Bay, is cool, airy and well proportioned.

A PLEASANT SUMMER RESIDENCE.
TERMS :—$1.00 to $1.50 per day, according to location. Special Rates for Summer Residents.

H. COWAN, - - - Proprietor.

NORTH AMERICAN HOTEL,
BRACEBRIDGE, MUSKOKA.

J. AVERY, - - Proprietor.

Every attention to Tourists and Pleasure Seekers.
Superior Accommodation to the General Public.

HUNTER, ROSE & CO.,

PRINTERS,

BOOKBINDERS, PUBLISHERS,

PAPER RULERS,

BLANK BOOK MANUFACTURERS,

ELECTROTYPERS AND STEREOTYPERS,

25 Wellington Street West,

TORONTO.

NIAGARA FALLS, NEW YORK.	NIAGARA FALLS, NEW YORK.
CATARACT HOUSE.	**INTERNATIONAL HOTEL,**
Spacious Parlours overlooking the Rapids.	ADJOINING THE NATIONAL PARK.
CURRENT BATHS.	Broad Piazzas and Fine Shade Trees.
THE LEADING HOTEL.	ALL MODERN EQUIPMENTS.
WHITNEY & JERRAULD, PROPRIETORS.	GLUCK, WARE & DELANO, PROPRIETORS.

INDIA RUBBER GOODS

OF EVERY DESCRIPTION.

:0:

The Largest and Only Complete Stock in the Dominion,

COMPRISING THE FOLLOWING:

Rubber Sportsman's Boots.
" Knee Boots.
" Fishing Stockings.
" Wading Pants and Boots combined.
" Gun Covers.
" Air Pillows and Air Beds
" Life Preservers (the latest invention).
" Water Bottles.
" Gas Bags.
" Nursery Sheeting.
" Clothing (of all kinds.)
" Horse Covers and Waggon Aprons.
" Gloves (the greatest invention of the age, price only $1.50 per pair.

Rubber Mats.
" Syringes.
" Bands and Rings.
" Hat and Caps.
" Leggings.
Ladies' Gossamer Circulars and Cloaks, from the very cheapest to the very best.
Rubber Ice Bags.
" Cotton and Linen Hose.
" Packing (all kinds).
" Lawn Hose (over 75,000 feet in stock).
" Car and Waggon Springs
" Gaskets and Rings.
" Valves.
" Buckets and Pails.
" Wringer Rolls.

RUBBER BELTING, PACKING AND HOSE.
RUBBER, COTTON AND LINEN HOSE.

Go to the great Rubber Warehouse for genuine goods such as are sold by an exclusive Rubber Store.

THE TORONTO RUBBER COMPANY,

AGENTS FOR THE GUTTA PERCHA AND RUBBER MF'G. CO'Y.

WAREHOUSE:

(MANNING ARCADE) - *KING STREET WEST,*

TORONTO.

They are features eminently picturesque, combining the aspects of wildness with the impression of exuberant fertility, and of boundless wealth.

Peaceful may they ever both remain.

The Niagara River, along the Canadian Side.

The Michigan Central R. R., after crossing the river near Black Rock on the International Bridge, skirts the bank, and passing "Falls View" as previously described, reaches the Niagara Falls station, within a stone's throw of the Clifton House, Wesley Park and the river banks. Two miles nearer Lake Ontario is *Clifton* or Suspension Bridge, where are the suspension and cantilever bridges and the junction with the Erie R. R. Soon the track, after running alongside the Grand Trunk R. R. for a few miles, dips suddenly under and, emerging, begins to wind slowly down the mountain side. Far below lie, laid out before the eye, the fertile and well tilled farms of fruit and grain, orchards and sheep-dotted pastures of the "Garden District of Canada;" above, upon the summit ridge, boldly stands out against the sky Brock's Monument. Having reached the lower level the train runs through a succession of vineyards and peach groves and gains the river at

NIAGARA-ON-THE-LAKE.

Alongside the dock are the steamers of the Niagara Navigation Company. This old town, in early days called *Newark*, was once the seat of Government and the Capital of Upper Canada whose first Parliament used to here hold its sittings. Now it is principally a place of summer resort. Upon the bluff headland facing the fresh breezes of the Lake is the "Queen's Royal Hotel," a first-class house kept in first-class style, by the proprietors of the "Queen's Hotel," Toronto. A capital beach for bathing, unlimited fishing—celebrated for enormous "bass,"—good boating, excellent roads and pleasant

THE QUEEN'S ROYAL HOTEL.

drives in a surrounding district of romantic and historic interest make a stay at "Niagara-on-the-Lake" most enjoyable. The Saturday evening "Hops" at the hotel are largely patronized by the resident American and Canadian Garrisons and the squadrons of the

"Royal Canadian" and "Toronto" Yacht Clubs are constant visitors. Many visitors from the Southern States spend their summer here and the Canadian Chatauqua holds its meetings in a large pavilion not far from the hotel

There are many pleasant private residences in the town, and the steamers of the Navigation Company keeping up a swift and constant service the "Society" of Toronto moves out *en masse* during the summer, so that Niagara-on-the-Lake has become almost a suburb of that city.

On the opposite bank of the river is *Youngstown*, with pleasant groves for picnicers and the headquarters and rifle ranges of the American forces of the Buffalo District, whose barracks are in the white-walled *Fort Niagara*.

The Battle of "Queenston Heights."

The surroundings of Niagara teem with historic reminiscences. Here sat the first Parliament of Canada, meeting in primitive simplicity beneath the shade of a spreading oak. Here were the headquarters of the garrison, and gallant soldier courted pretty maid in the festive days of the Capital of Upper Canada. But there were more stirring scenes than these, and deeds of valour took the place of sports of love.

Among the renowned of the many strifes along the River was the battle of Queenston Heights—fought on the 13th of October, 1812. The two countries had drifted into war; and on the morning of the 11th the Americans assembled a strong force at Lewiston, under General Rensselaer, with a view of making an attack upon Queenston. In addition to 800 men in garrison at Fort Niagara, there were 5,300 men under his command along the banks of the river. The Canadian force on the Western bank consisted of 1500 men, including Indians. Early on the morning of Tuesday, the 13th, their troops put off in thirteen boats and boldly crossed the rapid river, covered by a battery of two 18, two 6-pounders, and two field pieces, which they had placed on the high bank to the left of where the hotel now stands completely commanding every part of the opposite shore from which a landing could be effectually opposed. The Canadian batteries were one 18-pounder, high up on the Queenston Heights, and another 24-pound carronade, placed a little below the village, at Vrooman's Point. Three of the boats put back, while the remaining ten struck the shore a little above the village, and then returned for more troops. The Canadian force in Queenston consisted of two companies of the 49th Regiment and the "York Volunteer Militia"—altogether about 300 men. These, under Captain Dennis, advanced with a 3-pounder against the first division of the enemy under Colonel Van Rensselaer, who had formed his men near the river and was awaiting the arrival of the next boats. The Americans were driven with some loss behind a steep bank close to the water's edge, where they were reinforced with a fresh supply of troops, and returned the fire of the Canadians, who, stationed on the brow of the hill, fired down upon them.

A turn now took place in the course of the battle, for a strong detachment of the Americans, under Captain Wool, passing unperceived around a point of the river, ascended the rocks by a path which had been considered impassable, and gaining the crest of the Heights thus took the 18-pounder battery in rear. Captain Dennis was now compelled, with considerable loss, to retire to the village.

Meantime Sir Isaac Brock, in Niagara, hearing the cannonade, and

WHERE WOOL LANDED.

thinking that the attack at Queenston was only a feint to draw the garrison out of Fort George which was then to be attacked by the main body of the Americans, whom, he understood, were concealed in boats around the point on which Fort Niagara stands, determined to ride out himself and see how matters were before moving any of his troops.

Arriving with his two aides-de-camp at Queenston, he found the Americans—who had in the interval been strongly reinforced, and were about 1,000 in number—in possession of the Heights. Orders were despatched to General Sheaffe to bring up reinforcements from Fort George and to bombard Fort Niagara, which latter was done with such effect that its fire was silenced, and it was abandoned by its garrison. Although his available force numbered but 300, General Brock determined to retake the Heights, and, dismounting, charged at the head of his men. With impetuous rush, and despite the superior numbers, the hill was being carried !

But now the gallant Brock, struck by a bullet in the breast, fell near a thorn-bush, which marks the spot, and giving his last order, " Push on the York Volunteers !" lived only long enough to express the wish that his fall might not be made known to his men. Gallantly breasting the Height, his aide-de-camp, Lieutenant-Colonel Macdonell, the Attorney-General of the Province, next was mortally wounded when charging on up the hill and leading the York Volunteers. The battery was retaken, the 18-pounder spiked, and the Americans driven back to the edge of the cliff. Here some of their officers, hoisting a handkerchief upon a bayonet, were about to surrender, when Captain Wool valiantly tore it off, and, re-animating his men, opened a heavy fire. Inferior in numbers, their leaders fallen, and one-third of their men killed or wounded, the Canadians were now again compelled to retire, taking with them the body of the General, to the village of Queenston, there to await the expected assistance.

The Americans remained in quiet possession of the Heights for some hours, during which they did not receive many reinforcements, the events of the morning which had gone on in full view before their eyes, and the return to their side of many of the wounded causing, on the part of those who were left behind, a general disinclination to come across to the support of their comrades.

General Sheaffe now arrived from Fort George with nearly 400 of the 41st Regiment, 300 Militia, and 250 Indians, and leaving two field pieces in front of Queenston for its protection, marched off to the right by a circuitous route, and thus getting to the crest of the heights on which the Americans were posted, took them in flank. In numbers the two sides were about equal, and the courage of both unquestioned. The onset again commenced. The Indians, being more active in ascending the hill and passing through the woods, came first into contact, and, being repulsed, fell back on the main body, when the whole, advancing at the charge with a cheer, the Americans, after a short resistance, gave way and fled down the hill towards the landing place. Some who attempted to escape into the woods were driven back by the Indians, and many, cut off in their retreat, clinging to the bushes, went down the cliffs; some, losing their hold, were dashed upon the rocks beneath; and many others, reaching the river, perished in their attempt to swim across. The boats had been dispersed, the boatmen, panic stricken, having disappeared so that all retreat was cut off.

A flag of truce was now sent, and Brigadier Wadsworth and 950 men, surrendering unconditionally, were made prisoners.

All this proved the good results of General Brock's impetuous dash, for had the Americans not been attacked as they were, their reinforcements would have poured across the river and from their far superior numbers would have been able to over run the frontier.

The victory had been dearly gained by the loss of the General; and a three days' armistice to bury their dead being asked by the Americans, it was agreed to.

On the 15th General Brock was buried in one of the bastions of Fort George, with all military honours, and, with much generosity, minute guns, from the American Fort Niagara which had been reoccupied by its garrison, were fired during his funeral " as a mark of respect due to a brave enemy."

Such was the befitting close of the action so gallantly fought on both sides, and on condition of the Americans destroying their boats, which they at once did, the armistice was indefinitely prolonged. The Niagara was freed from the invader's presence and Brock rests in memory "The Saviour of his Country."

LINES ON THE DEATH OF BROCK.

As Fame alighted on the mountain's crest,
She loudly blew her trumpet's blast;
Ere she repeated Victory's notes she cast
A look around, and stopped: Of power bereft,
Her bosom heaved, her breath she drew with pain—
Her favourite *Brock* lay slaughtered on the plain !
Glory threw on his grave a laurel wreath,
And Fame proclaims, " A Hero sleeps beneath."
—*Bruyères.*

The Forts of Niagara.

The Forts, as now existing, are: On the American side, *Fort Niagara*, whose white walls tower over the meeting of the river and the lake; on the Canadian side, *Fort Missasaga*, whose decaying central tower peeps above the banks near the entrance of the river, and *Fort George*, whose bastions are barely recognizable in the grass-grown mounds into which their earthen walls have decayed, and crown the hill-tops just behind the steamboat landing. If for no other purpose, it would at least have been due to their historic past that these old monuments of gallant deeds should have been better cared for.

It will be interesting to note how often the sites of these fortifications have changed hands with the varying results of war.

THE EARLY STRUGGLES.

Happily these are times of peace; and the shores of this historic river are now given over to pleasure-seekers and the placid tillers of the soil. But in earlier days it was far different, and the mouth of the river, as commanding the best practicable route of transport between the East and West, was the scene of many a conflict.

The Indians—Senecas, Onondagas, Iroquois, and Missasagas—fought with one another for its possession, and against them all came the invading whites. As mourned Tecumseh,—

> "The Great Spirit gave
> The red men this wide continent as theirs,
> And in the East another to the white;
> But, not content at home, these crossed the sea,
> And drove our fathers from their ancient seats.
> Their sons in turn are driven to the lakes,
> And cannot further go unless they drown."—*Mair.*

THE FRENCH OCCUPATION.

The French, having entered the St. Lawrence in 1534, had, by means of the connecting waters of the Ottawa, extended their alliances with the natives in the region of the upper waters of Lakes Huron and Superior. For many years this was their sole route to the North-west, and it was not until 1669 that the southern route by the Niagara River and Lake Erie was discovered; and even then, as the shores were occupied by hostile tribes, they could not avail themselves of it. In 1684, the Northern tribes sent 500 of their warriors to the mouth of the Niagara River, there to meet the French forces, who, under Chevalier de la Barre, were to join them in occupying this, the central, point of their proposed new line of communication; but being intercepted on their way at Frontenac (now Kingston), by the Senecas and Iroquois—who occupied the southern shores of Lake Ontario—the French were beaten and retired again to Montreal, and their northern allies were then forced to return unsuccessful to their own countries.

In 1687 the French again advanced, and, having defeated the Senecas in a series of pitched battles—in which they were aided by the northern Indians from Mackinac—succeeded in erecting a wooden fort on the spot now occupied by the American Fort

Niagara. Scarcely had the main army retired than the garrison, under de la Troye, were hemmed in by the Senecas; and once more it passed into the hands of the Indians, but ten survivors of the whites escaping to tell the tale. It was again reoccupied, and, from a small log blockhouse seen during his travels in 1721 by Père Charlevoix, the French, under Joncaire, were, in 1726, permitted by treaty with the Senecas to enlarge the fort by adding four bastions, and to erect a storehouse. Meantime, the British colonies had established themselves at Oswego; and, the war between the British and French for the possession of the continent being in progress, Brigadier Prideaux was, in 1759, despatched with 2,500 men and 900 Indians, under Sir William Johnson, to capture Niagara. The account of the struggle is largely abridged from the excellent description given by Parkman in "Wolfe and Montcalm." The fort had been strongly rebuilt in regular form by Captain Pouchot, of the battalion of Béarn, and, being well supplied with munitions of war, was held by a garrison of 600, and assistance was expected from Detroit and the western French posts, under Aubrey.

On the 7th July the fort was invested from the land, and the lake was patrolled by numerous armed boats. The siege was begun in regular form, and by the 13th the British parallels had opened fire. The besieged contested every foot of the way, but their constant sallies were as constantly repulsed. On the 19th, the French schooner *Iroquois* attempted their relief, but was driven off by the British batteries, and the same night Prideaux was killed in the trenches while superintending the attack. The command devolved on Sir William Johnson, and in two or three weeks the fort was in extremity—the ramparts were breached, and many of the garrison slain. Pouchot watched anxiously for the promised succour; and on the morning of the 24th a distant firing told him they were at hand.

Aubrey and Ligneris had advanced to the rescue with 1,100 French and 1,200 Indians. To meet them, Johnson had been compelled to divide his forces into three separate bodies—one to guard the boats, one to guard the trenches, and one to fight Aubrey and his band. This last body placed themselves in ambush, and awaited the onset.

When Pouchot heard the firing, he went, with a wounded artillery officer, to the bastion next the river, and from here, by glimpses among trees and bushes, they descried bodies of men now advancing and now retreating—Indians in rapid movement, and the smoke of guns, the sound of which reached their ears in heavy volleys, or a sharp, angry rattle. Meanwhile the British cannon had ceased their fire, and the silent trenches seemed deserted, as if their occupants were gone to meet the advancing foe. There was a call in the fort for volunteers to sally and destroy the works; but no sooner did they show themselves along the covered way than the seemingly abandoned trenches were thronged with men and bayonets, and the attempt was given up. The distant firing ceased, and Pouchot remained in suspense. An Indian who had penetrated the lines told him that his friends had been defeated; but Pouchot would not believe him.

In the afternoon, after a furious cannonade on both sides, a trumpet sounded from the trenches, and an officer approached the fort, announcing the defeat, and with a summons to surrender. Still Pouchot would not believe, but, sending an officer of his own to the British camp, unanswerable proof was obtained; for there sat Ligneris, severely wounded, together with Aubrey and many others—nearly all the French officers, in their desperate efforts to retrieve the day, having been either killed or captured. An honourable capitulation was granted; and, in acknowledgment of their gallant defence, the garrison were allowed to march out with all the honours of war, and then lay down their arms upon the shores of the lake.

THE BRITISH OCCUPATION.

So passed away the power of the French in this district, for so great were the results of this victory that all their western posts, as far as Erie, surrendered without a struggle; and in 1763, by the Treaty of Paris, the whole of Canada and all the French possessions east of the Mississippi were ceded to the British crown.

THE NORTHERN LAKES OF CANADA.

For a long time the whole of the surrounding country was occupied solely by Indian tribes, so that during the war of 1776, although a small military post was maintained at Niagara by the British, no strife disturbed its quietude. By the treaty of peace of 1783, the east bank of the river was transferred to the United States, but Fort Niagara still continued to be held by a strong British garrison.

A settlement of U. E. Loyalists was now begun, and Paul Campbell, writing in 1791 of his visit there, says: "Opposite the fort of Niagara, on a large flat point on the Canadian side of the river, is a town lined out, and lots given *gratis* to such as will undertake to build on it agreeably to a plan laid down by Government, which, to me, seems to be a good one ; half an acre is allotted for the stance of each house and garden, and eight acres at a distance for enclosures, besides a large commonty reserved for the use of the town. Several pecle have taken lots here already, and no doubt, as the country advances in population so will the town in building. In the event of the fort on the opposite (American) side being given up, it is said there is one to be erected on this side, and the ground is already marked out for this purpose."

This town was *Newark*, afterwards changed to its present name of *Niagara*, and the fort was *Fort George*, which was constructed in 1792 — the following year—in such position that it should command *Fort Niagara*, the anchorage for shipping along the banks of the river, and the harbour within its mouth. *Fort Missasaga* was subsequently constructed to command the Canadian side of the mouth of the river, and any attacks which might be made from that quarter.

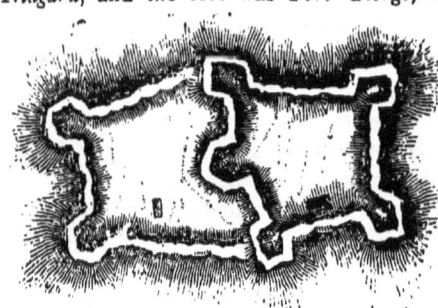
THE REMAINS OF FORT GEORGE.

Disturbances were threatening among the Indians of the west, and a council was called at Fort Niagara between their chiefs and representatives of the United States and Canadian Governments. Accordingly, in May, 1793, there arrived Benjamin Lincoln, Henry Randolph, and Timothy Pickering, the United States Commissioners. They were cordially received, and lodged in the fort. While awaiting the arrival of the delegates from the distant Indian tribes, it happened that, on the 24th of June, the birthday of King George of England was celebrated. Governor Simcoe gave an entertainment, ending with a ball in the evening. Thus it came about that the Commissioners, somewhat amusedly, found themselves guests celebrating a Royal gala day, with a Royal salute fired by a British garrison from a fortress on United States soil.

It is further said, that the meetings of the first Parliament of the Province of Upper Canada, which was summoned here in 1792, were held within the precincts of Fort Niagara.

Governor Simcoe, when, in that year, he first came to Canada supposed that the Government would still retain the possession of the fort, but he had his misgivings; and beginning to cast his eye about for another capital, which would not be "under the guns of an enemy's fort," selected the harbour on the north shore, then called Toronto, and occupied only by two families of Missasaga Indians— the French settlement at Fort Rouille having been abandoned by the French one hundred and fifty years before.

In 1795 the Duke de Liancourt visited Newark, and, telling of his stay at the humble wooden residence of Governor Simcoe, to which the sentries came daily from the fort across the river, says : " With very obliging politeness the Governor conducted me over the fort, which he is very loth to visit as he is sure he will be obliged to deliver it up to the Americans." Thirty artillerymen and eight companies of the Fifth Regiment then formed the garrison.

The seat of Government had, in 1793, been removed to Toronto, its name being changed to York ; and, under Jay's treaty, in 1794, the fort, together with those at Oswego, Detroit, Miami, and Michilimackinac, were to be given up. At length, no less than twenty years after the Revolution, on the 11th July, 1796, the last salute was fired to the red-cross flag as it was slow'y lowered from the flagstaff, and, the garrison and the guns being removed across the river to Fort George, Fort Niagara was finally handed over, and the stars and stripes floated peacefully above it until the war of 1812.

THE AMERICANS TAKE FORT GEORGE.

As previously mentioned, at the battle at Queenston Heights, in October, 1812, Fort Niagara was so vigorously assailed by Fort George that its garrison had to evacuate and retire from it. Possession was retaken upon the armistice, and again, in November, the two forts had an artillery duel which resulted in nothing but their mutual damage, without superior advantage to either. Matters remained quiet during the winter, but in the spring the Americans—collecting together a large number of ships and boats, and a force of soldiers and seamen—embarked in the early morning of the 27th May, 1813, and, under cover of a fog, crept down the Canadian shore. The battery, which occupied the site of the present Fort Missasaga, and near the lighthouse, which was then on the point, was first attacked, and was silenced by the weight of superior artillery; and after a gallant struggle the forlorn hope of 500 men forced a landing at a creek about a mile to the west. The Canadians, on the level plain, were shot down by the fire from the ships, while the landing parties—being protected by the high, overhanging banks—effected their landing on the beach. Reinforced from the fleet, they advanced —4,000 in number—upon Fort George, which General Vincent, being satisfied that the victory of the Americans was complete, evacuated, having spiked the guns and blown up all of the magazines, and retired with the remnants of his force to St. David.

The Americans remained in possession of Fort George all through the summer, during which a series of engagements took place with the result that they were hemmed in on all sides, and their supplies cut off. At length, on 10th December, 1813, upon the advance of the Canadian forces, under Colonel Murray, they evacuated Fort George, having first set fire to all the houses in Newark, rendering

FORT NIAGARA, FORT GEORGE, AND THE NIAGARA RIVER, IN 1813.

all the inhabitants — including the women and children —homeless and houseless in mid-winter.

Murray's advance was so swift that the retreat was precipitate, so much so that tents for 1,500 of the American garrison were left standing, and the fort itself undamaged.

THE CANADIANS RE-TAKE FORT NIAGARA.

Aroused to avenge the burning of the town, Murray, under the command of General Riall, on the night of the 18th December crossed the river, about three miles up, with 550 men, advancing stealthily at dawn, with bayonets fixed, and not a musket loaded lest by any chance an alarm might be given. The outlying picquets were surprised, and bayoneted to a man. Rushing forward, the walls were scaled with scaling-ladders, the interior gained, the main gate carried; and after a gallant resistance by the garrison, of whom 65 were killed and 12 wounded, at 5.30 in the morning Fort Niagara was once more in British possession. The American flag was sent as a trophy to the Governor-General at Montreal, and the Red-Cross floated again on both sides of the mouth of the river. Matters so continued until peace was declared, in February, 1815, when once more Fort Niagara was gracefully given up; and again, and in peace, the stars and stripes took the place of the redcross Jack.

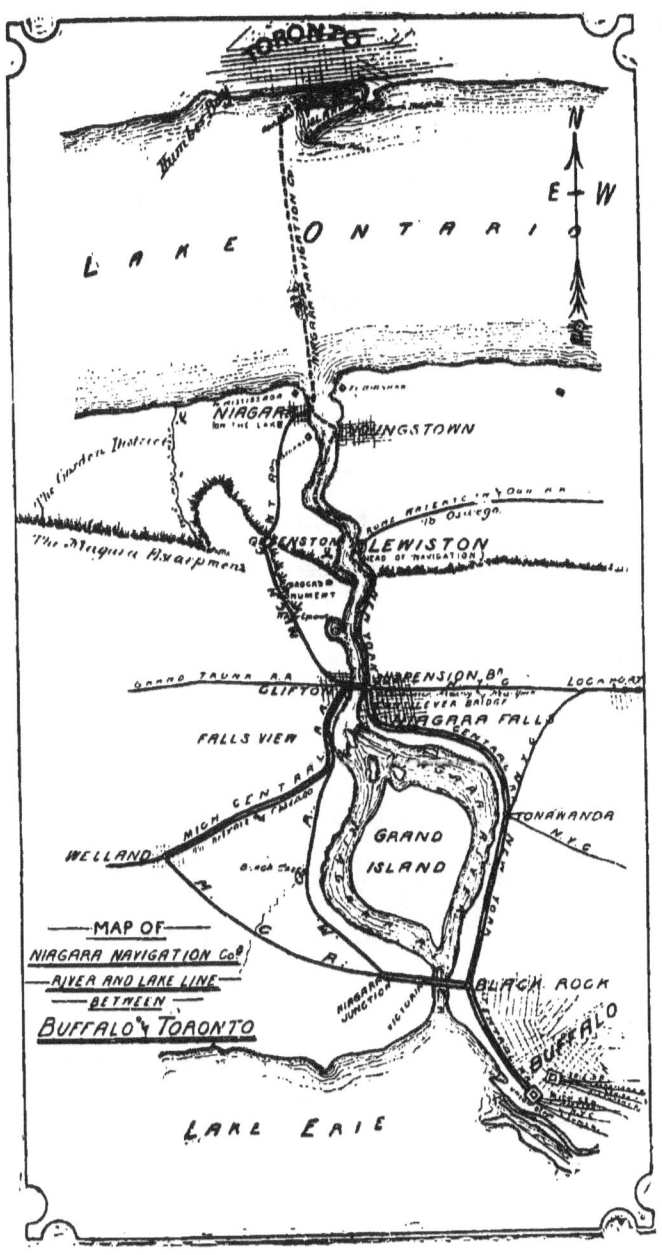

Thus had three nationalities—the French, the British, and the United States—been in successive possession of the fortifications that crowned this ancient point of land.

Twice had British valour stormed the ramparts, and from each of the others had it in turn wrested their possession at the bayonet's point—each time again retiring in honour to cede them as an evidence of national good-will.

The dismantled forts on the Canadian side, and the reverberating " sun-set gun " from the American fort, mark the continuance of the era of better days, wherein all strife upon these so oft-disturbed and still so hallowed shores has found an end; and their guardians now are rivals only in the arts of peace.

Lake Ontario.

This lake, the last of the series before the St. Lawrence proper is reached, is 180 miles long, and 234 feet above the sea. At this point the breadth between Niagara and Toronto is 35 miles, and is crossed in about two hours. The passage across the lake, in the middle portion of which the steamer is for a short time out of sight of land, gives full advantage of the pure cool winds which in summer fan its surface, and make the trip over and back one of the most attractive routes for those going from the districts south or west of Buffalo, to or from Toronto, and a great resort for the citizens of the city itself.

The palace steamer CHICORA, of the *Niagara Navigation Company*, is the largest steamer on the lake, is built of iron and steel, and is of the strongest and most substantial character. Of regular ocean-going style—having been built on the Clyde, and crossed the Atlantic—she maintains exact regularity of service in all weathers; and as old Boreas sometimes wakes up and develops a " snorter," it is well, therefore, to have a good bridge to carry one across. But these displays are only fitful in their occurrence, calm weather being the average from June to September. In olden days the crossing used to be made in from four to six hours, and communication—before the days of railways—was kept up the year round, the passengers being landed on the ice which fringed the shores. On the doors of the warehouses at Niagara are still to be seen the names of some of the old time vessels that occupied the route.

The *Chicora* is 230 feet long, with two raking funnels, and a generally "rakish" appearance. The *Entrance Saloon* is laid with maple and walnut; and a handsome circular staircase, with richly twisted railings, leads to the *Deck Saloon*. This unique apartment occupies the centre of the promenade deck, and is surrounded by windows giving a complete view and complete protection in rainy

STEAMER CHICORA.

weather. The *Promenade Deck* extends the full length of the steamer, so that a walk of a mile is obtained without much difficulty. Seats and comfortable arm chairs are provided in abundance, so that every opportunity is afforded for making a pleasant trip. The *Bar* is supplied by the Company with the choicest brands, and in the *Restaurant* meals are supplied while crossing the lake.

The *Marine Double Oscillating Engines*, built by the celebrated marine engineers, Messrs. Fawcett, Preston & Co., and the like of which are not in any other steamer on fresh water, are objects of much interest and admiration to visitors.

This steamer, leaving Toronto each week-day at 7 A.M. and 2 P.M., and Lewiston at 11 A.M. and 4.30 P.M., makes two trips each day, calling both ways at Niagara-on-the-Lake, and giving a pleasant outing on the open water of Lake Ontario, with the run of fourteen miles up and down the charming Niagara River. Direct connections are made, and through tickets issued in connection with all the Trunk Line Railways of the United States and Canada, and with the Royal Mail Line for the Thousand Islands and the Rapids of the St. Lawrence. Baggage requiring to pass Customs is examined by Customs officers on board the steamer while crossing the lake. (*S'e Advt*).

THE ISLAND—TORONTO.

When approaching Toronto from the southern shore, the light-house, on *Gibraltar Point*—the extreme west point of the island which forms and protects Toronto harbour—will be the first object to come in view. The island has been formed by the sands washing from the lofty Scarboro' Heights, which will be seen far away to the east. At one time it was possible to drive from the mainland along the Island, but ten years ago a breach was made at *Ashbridge's Bay*, which has since enlarged, and a permanent opening has from that time existed. The form of the island is being constantly changed. The lighthouse, when first erected, was within a few feet of the water; now it is a considerable distance inland, the sand having been constantly deposited here and on the long spits forming the west side of the protection of the harbour. A large and increasing population of summer visitors from the city is in occupation of the many slight but pretty houses erected all along the shores. A plank walk follows the beach the whole circuit of the island, and a steam tramway will soon be in operation.

Hanlan, the champion oarsman of the world, was born on this island, and the prominent building with high gables is his hotel, where can be seen the trophies of his prowess which he has won in all quarters of the globe. Bands play every evening in the summer in front of the hotel; and roller-coasters and merry-go-rounds make this the Coney Island of Torontonians. Ferries run to all parts of the island every few minutes.

The *Exhibition Buildings* attract the eye to the west, on the mainland, the white buildings in front of them, and close to the shore, are the barracks of the *New Fort*. Near here the American forces landed in 1813, and, after meeting with considerable resistance, they stormed the *Old Fort*, which may be noticed on the shore close to the entrance of the harbour. The Canadian garrison, being inferior in numbers, and unable to withstand the attack, retreated, and, in doing so, blew up their magazine, by which the American commander, General Pike, and 200 of his men were killed, and many wounded. The spot where this occurred is just a little to the west of the present parapet.

Toronto slopes very gently upwards from the water's edge, so gently as to present an almost level apppearance. The sky line is broken by the spires and towers of the churches and other buildings, and a fringe of green from the trees surmounting the *Davenport Hills*, which are the north limit of the city, forms a setting to the whole.

Baggage is claimed on board, and transferred by the Toronto Transfer Company to the several hotels or railway stations.

The Royal Mail Line Steamers, for the Rapids of the St. Lawrence and Montreal, leave from the same dock.

Toronto as a Summer Resort.

This city has gradually become the acknowledged centre for the Province of Ontario, of intellectual study, political opinion, legal research and monied influence—all potent motives to attract residents to settle within its borders. But beyond and in addition to these are the lighter and more enjoyable attractions of amusement and relaxation that serve to lighten the labour of anxious business, and while away the hours for persons of leisure.

Theatres, concert halls, parks, and (if they may be enumerated in the class of mental relaxations) sensational preachers of much power, are adjuncts that may be added to any city, wherever its location.

In these respects Toronto is amply endowed. She has, however, a natural endowment in her geographical and physical position and of which she is now only beginning to avail herself; these advantages have contributed not a little to her past improvement, and bid fair to aid her happily in her advance towards metropolitan greatness. This city is pre-eminently a lakeside resort. In the past the streets have, and unless the city fathers should with infinite blindness to her own good, and with poor faithlessness in their future expansion, adopt an opposite policy, will for all time give open and unrestricted access to the waters of the harbour. No resident of, or visitor to, Toronto but can—either by street-car or a short walk—get down to the water side, and enjoy a balmy evening's row upon the sheltered waters of the bay, reaching home again at an early hour, and retire to rest invigorated by manly exercise and health-giving air. In the evenings the waters of the harbour are fairly alive with boats. Take any city of similar size, and beyond all doubt there are more pleasure boats to the aggregate number of families in Toronto than anywhere else on the globe. It is said there are cities in China where a large number of people live in houses floating on the water; but any one who saw the welcome given to Edward Hanlan—the Patron Saint of Toronto Bay—when he came home crowned with the laurels of victory, and all the water was covered with multitudinous craft of every size and shape, from the stately *Chicora* to the veriest "dug-out," would have said, "Here is a whole city all afloat." And so it is; the people of Toronto are the most persistent water lovers—for corroborative evidence see the puffing ferries carrying their teeming loads of laughing children and anxious mothers to the sandy beaches of the island; see the evening moonlight excursions, when, to the light of the moon and the strains of merry music, the maidens and their swains dance the soft summer hours away; see the Saturday afternoon excursions, when steamer after steamer leaves the docks for neighbouring lakeside parks, for "luscious" Oakville, "ambitious" Hamilton, or "historic," delightful Niagara.

By common consent the Canadian business world has agreed that "All work and no play makes Jack a dull boy," and while our neighbours in the States may dig and delve, may sweat and strain in the ceaseless struggle for dollars and gain, we in Canada will pause awhile in the quick pursuit, and cultivating that more intelligent view of the work of man, let our youth sally forth to open air, fresh fields, athletic sports and vigorous play, setting their systems all aglow with vigorous health, and mind and brain re-invigorated and better fitted for week day work again. It is this opportunity of enjoyment, and this spirit of taking advantage of the opportunity, that has attracted to Toronto many people from other parts of Canada, and in fact from the world at large to become permanent residents.

Cool lakeside breezes in summer and temperate moderation of cold in winter, make Toronto a very pleasant place in which to live, and the progress of the past proves it also to be a very good place in which to thrive.

The City of Toronto.

NAME AND EARLY HISTORY.

The Capital of Ontario is perhaps the most progressive and promising City in Canada. Even now it may be considered to be only in its youth, as there are still living within its borders inhabitants who can remember when there were but two or three brick houses, and they, and the few shanties which comprised the village, were hemmed together in a small clearing cut from the surrounding forest.

The earliest mention of the name is found among some French memoirs in 1686, in connection with the "*Portage of Toronto.*" The country in the neighbourhood of what is now called Lake Simcoe, appears then to have been known as the "Toronto region," a region "well peopled," and a great "place of meeting," which is the most probable signification of the word. The portage to this place of meeting began at the protected harbour on the shores of the lake, thence by the Humber river, then called the *Toronto river*, and then by a trail to the interior. In course of time a fort was erected by the French, at the Lake Ontario end of the trail, the remains of which are to be seen in the grounds of the *Exhibition Buildings*. This at first, called Fort Rouillé, afterwards came to be called Fort Toronto, and thus the general name of the interior country came to be localized in this one vicinity and applied to the village which sprung up on the shores of the bay.

In 1793 the seat of government of the Province was removed from Niagara to Toronto, and the name of the latter then changed to "York," in compliment to Frederick, Duke of York, the son of the then reigning King, George III.

The new name of York never seems to have fitted smoothly to the tongue or to have thoroughly settled down upon the place.

In 1801 the Poet Moore, writing "from the banks of the St. Lawrence," most probably from St. Anne's, when he composed the undying "Canadian Boat Song," adheres to the musical cadence of the old and cherished name.

> " I dreamt not then that ere the rolling year
> Had filled its circle, I should wander here
> In musing awe ; should tread this wondrous world.
> See all its store of inland waters hurled
> In one vast volume down Niagara's steep,
> Or calm behold them, in transparent sleep,
> Where the blue hills of old Toronto shed
> Their evening shadows o'er Ontario's bed."

In 1834, on the occasion of the community having arrived at the size and dignity of a "City," the old name of *Toronto* was once more enthusiastically revived and officially renewed.

In 1794 there were 12 houses in the village, in 1812 its population was 900, in 1879, 71,000, and now the little " place of meeting," has grown to be a city of 130,000 inhabitants, a rate of progress of which any community might well be proud.

THE NORTHERN LAKES OF CANADA.

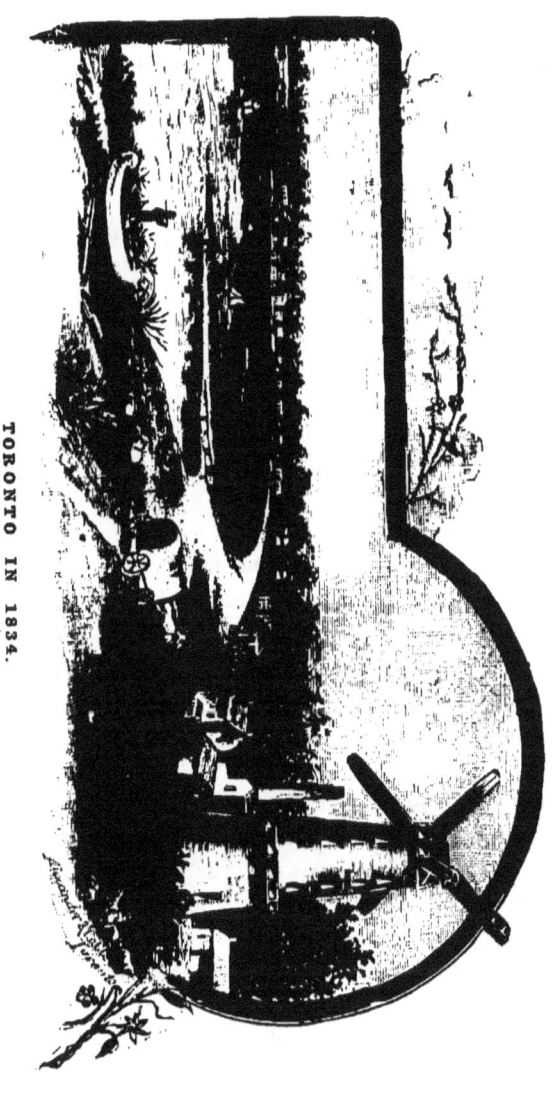

TORONTO IN 1834.

The hotel accommodation is ample for the largest gatherings, hence Toronto is now more than ever a favourite "place of meeting," and as in olden days the Indian tribes came here together, so now, headed by their Chiefs and Patriarchs, come the brethren of the various social, benevolent, or business organizations from all parts of the Continent.

The Rossin and Queen's ($2.00 to $4.00), Walker and American ($2.00), Albion, Russell, Revere, ($1.50), may be mentioned as among the best. *(See advts.)*

KING STREET.

The Town was first established on the banks of the river Don, at the head of the harbour, and in the far east end of the present city. At the shores of this river begins King, the east and west entry of the city, the main street of the original village, as it is now of the grown up community.

Upon the site where now exists the unattractive but massive stone proportions of the "OLD GAOL," stood the original and first *Houses of Parliament* of the Province of Upper Canada. The Buildings were of wood and not of very imposing character, but they contained "two elegant halls," for the accomodation of the Legislature and the Courts of Justice.

At the time of the American foray in 1813, these, together with the library and all the papers and records, were burned, the church was robbed and the town library pillaged. Strangely enough the Public Buildings at Washington, were a few months afterwards destroyed by a British force, and this was considered at the time a fair reparation for the damages effected at Toronto.

The town market-place used to be in the block between the St. Lawrence Hall and Church street, opposite where St. James' Cathedral now stands. The land is still the property of the city, and the revenue from the ground leases contributes to decrease the taxation of the citizens.

Here, as late as 1834, the stocks and pillory used to be set up; and it is on record that a certain Elizabeth Ellis was, for "being a nuisance," condemned to stand in this pillory for two hours on each of two market days. Seeing that these ancient instruments of punishment have long since been removed, we may be satisfied that the ladies of this fair city are now free from any such imputation ; indeed, any one who makes his afternoon stroll along the fashionable strolling grounds, that is to say, between Church and York streets, on the south side of King street, at the fashionable hour of four in the afternoon—particularly on Saturday afternoons—will see such glimpses of beauty, combined with bright complexions and hearty healthfulness, that he will admit the justice of the reputation for pretty faces and good nature which is so widely conceded to the young ladies of Toronto.

King street continues westward, lined by the best of the retail stores, and after penetrating *Parkdale*—the "flowery suburb"—loses itself upon the banks of the *Humber Bay*, thus connecting together the two rivers which, east and west, bound the plateau upon which the city is built.

YONGE STREET.

The streets of Toronto are all laid out at right angles to one another. This, no doubt, takes away from its picturesqueness, but contributes to its convenience, as, once the bearings of the compass have been ascertained, the visitor can scarcely lose his way. Roughly speaking, the water side is to the south ; the streets starting from the Bay run north—the others, crossing them, run east and west. They are all of good width, many are block-paved and boulevarded, and most are fringed with trees—a feature which in time will add greatly to their appearance.

Yonge street, at the foot of which the steamers land, is perhaps the longest street in the world ; at all events, the palm is given to it by George Augustus Sala in his " Streets of the World." It was projected in 1793 to form a "portage to the upper lakes without the necessity of going up Lake Erie, and passing Detroit."

The intersection of King and Yonge streets may be taken to be the centre of the city's life, and forms a sort of *Quatre-voies*, or *Four Crossway*, from which a starting point may well be made.

Forty years ago, Yonge street, between King and Queen streets, was well-nigh impassable; and when the road-bed was excavated for the present block pavement, remnants were still found of the old corduroy road which once served to keep the ox-carts of the early settlers afloat through this slough of Despond. A good tanner named Jesse Ketchum then lived alongside, and his name is here perpetuated by the "Bible House," the ground on which it stands having been given by him to the "Bible and Tract Society" on condition that they would annually expend the amount of the ground rent in Bibles, and distribute them to scholars in the public schools—an annual ceremonial which is never omitted, and always is productive of great interest.

Built as a Government work, for forty-six miles Yonge street became the main artery for settlements to the north, its roadsides soon were lined with the houses of settlers, and the name of "street" thereby justified. An early incident is pleasantly embalmed in "Toronto of Old," that "A story is told of a tourist, newly arrived at York, wishing to utilize a stroll before breakfast by making out as he went along the whereabouts of a gentleman to whom he had a letter. Passing down the hall of his hotel, he asked in a casual way, of the book-keeper, 'Can you tell me where Mr. So-and-so lives?' (leisurely producing the note from his breast pocket); 'it is somewhere along Yonge street here in your town.' 'Oh, yes,' was the reply, when the address had been glanced at; 'Mr. So-and-so lives on Yonge street, about twenty-five miles up!'"

Having now got the bearings of the two main arteries, we may wander more at large.

Map of Toronto.

Showing the principal streets and public buildings.

(Street Car Routes are marked in dotted lines.)

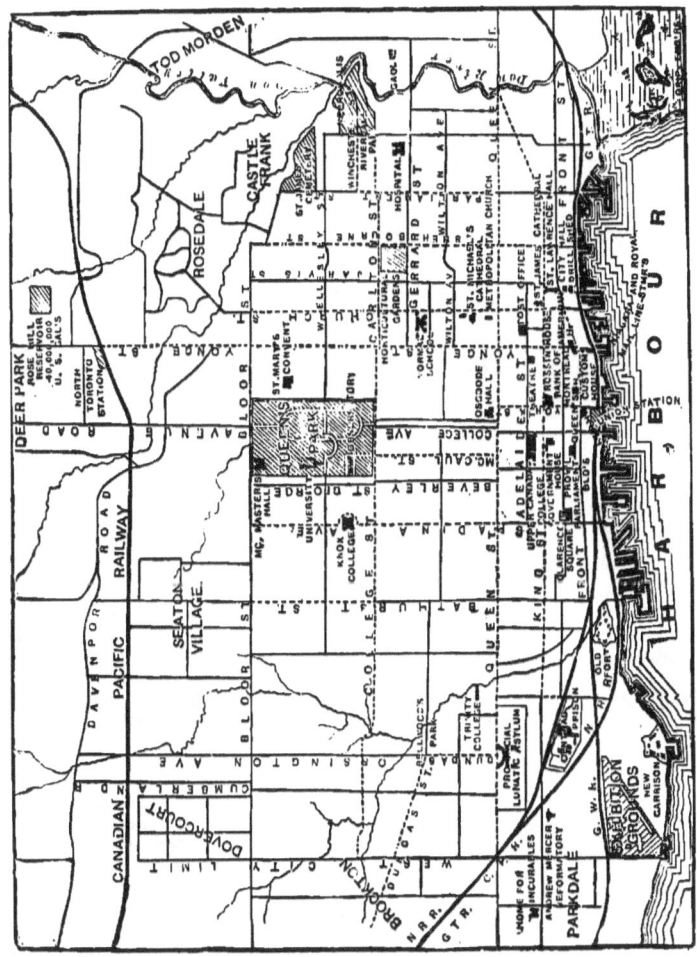

STREET CARS.

The street car system is being rapidly extended, and is even now such that with a little consideration all parts of the city can be reached by their means. The routes covered are shown in the attached plan of the city, and the cars are plainly marked with the names of the principal streets along which they run. Fare for continuous trip, 5c.; six fares, 25c.

The Street Car Routes.

CARS MARKED.	COLOUR LIGHT.	STARTING POINT.	ROUTE.
King	Blue.	Don Bridge.	King to Strachan Avenue.
Yonge..	Red.	Market.	King, Yonge to North Toronto Station.
Queen	White.	"	King, Yonge, Queen West to Parkdale.
Queen & Brockton.	Green.	"	King, Yonge, Queen west, Dundas St. to Dundas Bridge.
McCaul & College.	Red and Blue	"	King, York, Queen McCaul, College.
Spadina Avenue to Seaton Village.	Yellow.	"	King, Spadina Ave., College, Bathurst to Bloor.
Spadina Avenue to Bloor.	Red & Green.	"	King, Spadina Ave. to Bloor.
Queen East.	White.	Union Station	Front, Yonge, Queen to Don Bridge.
Yonge St. to North Toronto.	Red.	"	Front, Yonge to North Toronto.
Church.	Blue.	"	Front, Church to Bloor.
Sherbourne.	Red.	"	York, King, Sherbourne to Bloor
Sherbourne.	Red.	"	Front, Church, Queen, Sherbourne to Bloor.
Winchester.	Green.	"	Front, Church, King, Sherborne, Carlton, Parliament, Winchester.
Parliament.	White.	"	Front, Church, King, Sherborne, Queen, Parliament and Gerrard St. east.
College Ave. and Carlton St.	White.	Across town.	College St., College Ave., Carlton, Parliament.

CABS.

Cabs can be obtained on the public stands or from the principal livery stables—by telephone from the hotels.—(*See Advertisements*).

The usual rate is $1 per hour, within the city limits, for one to four persons. The drivers and vehicles are all licensed under police supervision, and incivility or overcharges are very seldom met with. In taking a drive around the city or its environs, the pleasantest way for driver and for passenger is to come to an understanding about the rate *before starting.*

DRIVES.

In addition to the usual drives through the main streets to visit the several public buildings, the following drives may be mentioned as giving good examples of the pretty country surrounding the city.

Distances out and back from Corner of King and Yonge streets.

EAST—The Lake Shore Road, Woodbine, Ben Lamond, Don and Danforth Road, and the Necropolis—8½ miles.

NORTH-EAST—Necropolis, Todmorden, Don Valley, Eglinton, Mount Pleasant— 6½miles.

NORTH—Queen's Park, Deer Park, Ridge Road, St. Albans street, St. George street—6 miles.

NORTH-WEST—College street, Bloor street, Slattery's, High Park, Queen street, and Subway—8½ miles.

WEST—King street, Lake Shore Road, Humber Bay and back—9 miles.

THE PUBLIC BUILDINGS.

The public buildings of Toronto are of singular excellence, and are really well worth visiting both for their architectural value and the instructive and interesting character of their contents. The more important are here mentioned, somewhat in the order in which they may be visited during a drive through the city.

Front street, running parallel with the harbour, is lined with handsome wholesale warehouses.

THE NORTHERN LAKES OF CANADA.

UNION STATION.

UNION STATION.—Upon the Esplanade which skirts the water's edge, all the railways enter the city, and focus their radiations in this station. In 1851 the first sod of the Ontario, Simcoe and Huron Railway (the first railway in Ontario) was turned at a spot on the water's bank, not far from here. The ceremony was performed by the Countess of Elgin, in the presence of well nigh the whole town. Lord Elgin facetiously said "it may seem a singular application of the principle of division of labour, that the lady should dig and the gentleman speak. But this is an age of progress in which we must be prepared for much that is strange." He then adverted to the great advantages which would accrue from the construction of railways—predictions which have been fully verified.

It seems almost impossible to believe that so short a time ago this city was in the winter locked in from all communication except by sleigh, and that in the summer the only connection with the outer world was by water. Yet it was so, and some of the older boys can still remember the wonderment with which the first locomotives were viewed when they emerged from Jemmy Good's workshops, on Richmond street, and made their slow progress on temporary wooden tracks through the streets, down Yonge street to the Esplanade.

As contrast to this primitiveness there are now 77 trains, bearing and delivering passengers to all parts of the continent, daily entering the Union Station.

The visitor arriving by water will notice at the foot of Yonge street the CUSTOM HOUSE, of highly decorated Italian architecture. On the exterior are elaborate carvings of fruits and flowers, a well executed bust of the Queen, and alto-relievos of the most celebrated English navigators and seamen—Drake, Nelson, Jacques Cartier, Cook, and others. "The Long Room," where the public business is transacted, is most handsomely fitted and decorated.

On the opposite corner is the new and handsome *Bank of Montreal*, a good instance of the care of a thoughtful architect to preserve the unpurchaseable advantage of trees and foliage as an adornment to the structure itself. The octagonal counting-room within is admirably decorated with rare marbles and stained glass. The other Banks are mainly situated on *Wellington street*—the *Standard, Ontario*, and *Bank of Toronto* being well housed.

THE CUSTOM HOUSE.

Torontonians are proverbial as a church-going people, there being no less than 120 churches and chapels in the city, or almost one for every 1,000 inhabitants. Sunday in Toronto is really a day of rest. All saloons close at 7 on Saturday evening, and do not open again until Monday morning,—a law which is strictly observed. No street cars are run and scarcely a wheel of any kind turns. No business of any description is conducted and no shops are open. Yet the streets are full of people either going to and from church or visiting their friends. Thus Monday morning finds everyone reinvigorated and ready for their work. On the corner of Church and King street, the most important street of this city, is ST. JAMES' CATHEDRAL, the Seat of the Anglican Bishop of Toronto, a fine example of perpendicular Gothic architecture.

ST. JAMES' CATHEDRAL.

The spire, rising to the height of 316 feet, is gracefully proportioned, and the most lofty on the continent—exceeding that of Trinity Church, New York, by 21 feet. The tower contains a chime of bells and the celebrated clock manufactured by Benson, of London, which obtained the highest prize at the Vienna Exhibition.

In the interior, the apse, surrounded by fine traceried windows, is finely decorated in carved oak, and contains monuments to Bishop Strachan, the first Anglican Bishop in Canada, and Dean Grasett— both of whom, as also the wife of the Dean, are interred in the chancel—Chief-Justice Draper and others. The stained glass chancel windows—illustrating in the upper sections "The Ascension," and below, "The Last Supper," after Leonardo da Vinci; also in the east window "The Christian Virtues"—are fine examples of the best art work of Munich.

The tower and spire can be ascended; and in addition to seeing the works of the clock, a wide range of view can be had of the city, the harbour and surrounding country.

The present church is the fourth which has occupied the present site, its predecessors having been destroyed by fire.

The acoustic properties are peculiarly good, most probably due to the apsidal form of the chancel, so that the lowest tones are carried to the farthest extremity. Entrance is by the north-west door between 10 A.M. and 3 P.M. A fee of ten cents for ascending the tower is collected towards the cost of maintaining the clock and chimes.

A little further east on King street is the *St. Lawrence Hall*, with cupola and clocks, containing the principal markets and some municipal offices. The present home of the city officials is in the old *City Hall*, a little to the south; but a site has been purchased, and new city buildings and Court-House, to cost $500,000, are projected.

Church street used to be the extreme west end of the town and was so called from the first church, which occupied the corner of it and King, and was then entirely surrounded by the forest trees.

The Public Library, on the corner of *Adelaide street*, is the successful growth of but a few years. The number of books on its shelves in 1885 was 41,286; and as it is already attracting generous donations from private libraries, as being the fit receptacle for the custody and preservation of books valuable either for their rarity or their character, and where the benefit of their ownership may be shared with other less fortunate but yet congenial minds, its size will soon attain considerable proportions. A sum of about $4,000 per annum is expended on new purchases, and the Library has already an established reputation for its collection of books and documents bearing on early Canadian history. The number of books taken out by readers in 1885 was 277,931—a goodly proportion to the population of the city. A well-conducted Free Reading Room, stocked with the best periodicals and newspapers, is a favourite resort, and well attended.

Passing up *Church street*, next is seen the METROPOLITAN CHURCH, the headquarters of the Methodists of Canada. It is magnificently situated in the centre of an open square. The turreted tower and many pinnacles distinguish it from the other churches of the city. The organ is the largest in Canada, containing 3,315 pipes, and compares favourably with many noted organs in Europe—

METROPOLITAN CHURCH.

Metropolitan Church
  Organ, Toronto . . 53 Stops.
Strasbourg Cathedral 46 "
Temple Church, London, England . . . 47 "
Westminster Abbey . 32 "
Exeter Hall . . . . . . 42 "

The voicing and tone of the organ are of rare excellence; thus much attention is devoted to musical excellency and the choir of the church is of a high standard.

Next is the Roman Catholic *St. Michael's Cathedral*, the interior highly frescoed, and containing a very handsome east window in stained glass, representing "The Crucifixion." The Archbishop has here his official throne.

The Normal School is the centre of the Public School System of the Province. In it are the offices of the Minister of Education, and the Depository of books, &c., for distribution to the schools; and adjoining it are the *Model Schools* for boys and girls, in which the student teachers can see the school system in actual operation.

The gardens are kept in fine order, each plant there being labeled with its proper botanical name. In the interior is a really fine collection of paintings, comprising selections of originals and copies illustrating the great schools of art, copies of the most celebrated statues, and casts exhibiting the characteristic styles and ornaments of Gothic and Modern architecture. In the *Grand Central Hall* and around the *Theatre* are placed busts of the philosophers, orators and historic men of Roman and Grecian eras, the monarchs of England and eminent statesmen, authors, poets and celebrities of each reign. In the *Gallery of the Statues* are many examples of modern and ancient sculpture, among them Venus de Medicis, Urania, Cicero, Canova's Hebe, Powers' Greek Slave, Gibson's Homeless Wanderer, and Psyche borne by the Zephyrs, Thorwaldsen's Guardian Angel, &c. In the same room is a full series of impressions in wax from the seals of the Sovereigns of England, from the time of Edward the Confessor. A number of fine copies of portrait medallions and antique gems most interesting to those interested in gem cutting. In the next Gallery are examples of great educational value of the best varieties of maps, models for object lessons, philosophical apparatus, and generally of school equipment from which many useful ideas can be gleaned.

NORMAL SCHOOL.

The Picture Galleries occupy the whole front of the buildings and on their spacious walls *the Paintings* are splendidly displayed. The

Italian, Flemish, Dutch, German, French and Spanish Schools of Art are all represented. The pictures are all numbered and the following may be particularly mentioned :

13, "Peter's Denial of Christ," Gherardo. 35, "The Mother of Sorrows," Sassoferato, a painter celebrated for the beautiful shades of blue which usually appear in his portraits of the Virgin and of female saints. 15, "The Remorse of Peter," Carlo Dolci. 40, "Head of St. John presented to Herodias," Luini. 51, "The Grand Canal, Venice," Canaletti. Among some good examples of Guido Reni, whose grace and harmony of colouring are rarely excelled, are, 61, "Lucretia," a lady of ancient Rome distinguished for her beauty and virtue, who, resenting the outrage offered to her by Sextus Tarquin (B. C. 507), took own life. 63, "The Massacre of the Innocents." 62, "Beatrice Cenci." 60, "The Archangel Michael." 64, "Aurora," Goddess of the Morning (this last one is on the west stairway). 68, "The Last Communion of St. Jerome," Domenichino. 73, "The Conspiracy of Cataline," Salvator Rosa. 82, "Beatrice Cenci the Night Before Her Execution," A. Ratti (*See also* No. 62). The poet Shelley has dramatized, in his poem "The Cencis," the story of the wrongs of her who was

"Cut off
From light and life and love in youth's sweet prime."

23, "Madonna della Sedia," the only Madonna painted by Raphael who has not her eyes cast down. The original was painted upon the head of a cask. 32, "The Transfiguration," Raphael—by common consent his master-piece—which was placed over his head when he lay in state at his funeral obsequies. 30, "La Fornarina," portrait of the Roman maiden with whom Raphael fell in love. 2, "The Head of the Medusa," Leonardo da Vinci.

HOW PERSEUS BROUGHT BACK THE GORGON'S HEAD.

In the old Greek myth of Perseus and how he slew the Gorgon, to those who read beneath, there lies a deeper meaning than appears upon the surface. The goddess Athené inspires Perseus, a noble Greek youth, to brave deeds, leading him to feel it were "Better to die in the flower of youth, on the chance of winning a noble name, than to live at ease and die unloved and unrenowned." Having come to manhood's age she tests him to go forth and slay Medusa, the Gorgon, and bring back to her, as trophy, the foul one's head The Medusa had once been a maiden beautiful as morn, till in her pride she sinned a sin at which the sun hid his face ; and from that day her hair was turned to vipers and her hands to eagle's claws ; and her heart was filled with shame and rage, and her lips with bitter venom ; and her eyes became so terrible that whosoever looked upon them was turned to stone. Her children were the winged horse and the Giant of the golden sword, and her grandchildren Echidna, the witch-adder, and Geryon, who fed his herds beside the herds of hell. So she became the sister of the Gorgons, Stheino and Euryte the abhorred. Then Athené gave to Perseus her polished shield, in the reflected brass of which he was to look so that he might strike safely and not be turned to stone, and Hermes gave his sandals, on which quivered living wings, so that they might carry him unwearied safe over land and sea, and his sword of diamond of one clear precious stone, Herpé, the Argus-slayer. So Perseus sailed high over the mountain tops and skimmed over the billows like a sea-gull and his feet were never wetted, far away into the heart of the Unshapen Land, beyond the streams of Ocean, where there is neither night nor day, until he heard the rustle of the Gorgons' wings and saw the glitter of their brazen talons, and as he looked in the mirror of his shield he saw the three lying below him in their sleep with mighty wings outspread. And the Medusa tossed to and fro restlessly, and as she tossed Perseus pitied her. In her face still stayed the form of beauty, but her cheeks were pale as death and her brows were knit with everlasting pain, and her lips were thin and bitter like a snake's ; and around her temples the horrid vipers wreathed and, moving constantly, shot out their fiery tongues. But as he looked, Perseus saw, that for all her beauty the Medusa was as foul and venomous as those with whom she lay. With one stroke from Herpé the head was severed, and her wings and talons rattled as Medusa sank dead upon the rocks. And so, wrapped in a goatskin, Perseus bore back to Pallas Athené the Gorgon's head.

In Room No. 6, in the rotary stands, is a collection of over 600 photographs of *National Historical Portraits*, being taken from paintings of eminent persons from the time of the Plantagenets to the end of James II (1152 to 1688). The originals were exhibited at the first special exhibition of national portraits, at South Kensington Museum. They are classified and chronologically arranged and the names of the painters given when known. Other stands contain photographs of paintings in the National Gallery, England.

The Italian and Flemish schools are the best represented, and in the corridors are many excellent small examples of the Dutch school. In cases in the centres of the rooms are photographs of the Kings and Queens of England and of well-known men of Britain and Canada. In the "*Nineveh Gallery*," are copies from the great Layard collection of the British Museum.

There are many electrotypes of art treasures in the London South Kensington Museum—casts of gen. , medals, coins, etc. ; and altogether an Art collection of singular excellence.

Here school-boys and scholars will find materialized—either in picture or in sculpture—many of the personages or events with which they meet in their reading ; and if this collection were intelligently used and referred to, it would be found that much additional interest and zest would be given thereby to reading and to study. There is a good catalogue for sale at the office—price 25 cents. Entrance is free throughout the year from 9 A.M. to 5 P.M. on week-days, except on Christmas and New Year's days.

The private residences of Toronto present a genuine air of quiet and comfort, and in this district a very fair example may be seen of their character. On Jarvis street is the *Baptist Church*—one of the most picturesque in the city; the interior is of amphitheatrical form, thus giving great play of outline to the exterior, to which the Queenston brown stone, New Brunswick red granite, and ornamental

slates, add great colour and
effect. The organ is remarkable for the beauty of its tone.
THE HORTICULTURAL GARDENS occupy a square of ten
acres. During the summer a
beautiful display of flowers is
kept up, which is well worth
visiting—particularly the *Rosarium*, for its great variety of
roses. The grounds are the
property of the city, and entrance is free from 6 A.M. to
8 P.M. Band concerts and
exhibitions of fire-works are
given at frequent intervals in
the evenings, from the proceeds of which, together with
a grant from the city, the gardens are maintained. The
land was a liberal gift to his
native city by the Hon. Geo.

BAPTIST CHURCH.

W. Allan. The gardens were opened by His Royal Highness the
Prince of Wales in 1860; and a tree then planted by him now
exhibits considerable growth.

The Pavilion Music Hall occupies the west side of the gardens.
Attached to it are the conservatories, in which an excellent "winter
garden" is maintained. Having a seating accommodation for 3,000,
and excellent acoustic properties, it has been of great advantage to
the music-loving people of the city as an educator, and has given
opportunities for attracting the best exponents of the continent. The
Monday Popular Concerts, given here every fortnight throughout the
winter, and the annual festivals of the Philharmonic and Choral
Societies, are good evidences that a very high class of music culture

E

flourishes among the citizens. The best public balls are given in this Pavilion, for which it has unexampled facilities.

The *Boys' Home* and the *Girls' Home*, two excellent charities for the retreat and care of destitute children not convicted of crime, are in the vicinity, and invite visitors to view their work. The tall towers of *The General Hospital* are seen still further to the east.

This establishment is in every way a model, with its subdivisions for cure of the various classes of disease, eye and ear infirmary, lying-in hospital, etc., and separate convalescent and recreation wings.

Near by are its attendant schools of medicine. *Trinity School* taking its degrees from Trinity College and *Toronto School* from University College. The reputation of these schools is very high and their degrees greatly esteemed throughout the Continent, so that a college population of between 400 and 500 are in attendance at their lectures.

OSGOODE HALL.

Not far from King Street, and at the head of *York Street*, standing in ornamental grounds is *Osgoode Hall*, named after the first Chief Justice of Canada, and the seat of the Highest Law Courts of the Province. The interior surpasses that of any other Courts of Law, and is of rare beauty. The Central Court, of two stories in the Italian style is adorned with double rows of Doric columns in cream-coloured stone from Caën, in Normandy. The best view on the entrance floor is obtained from the extreme north-west corner, from where the several rows of columns can be brought into perspective. On the walls are portraits of the Chief-Justices and Chancellors; from the upper colonnade the Law Courts are entered—in each, above the seats of the Judges, a bas-relief of "Impartial Justice." The Library is a magnificent chamber, with lofty domed ceiling, and many-nooked bookshelves for the 30,000 volumes which it contains. A fire-place of fine design and proportions occupies the west end; over it the portrait of Chief-Justice Sir John Beverley Robinson, who, when a young man, served under General Brock, at the battle of Queenston Heights, in 1821. In the adjoining wings are the offices of the various Courts. The grounds are well kept.

The judges in Canada are not elected, but are appointed by the General Government, during "good behaviour," or practically for life; and as they are always selected from the first ranks of the profession, the Canadian Judiciary bears high record for talent and unimpeachable integrity.

Should any of the Courts be in session the visitor will be struck with the dignity and decorum with which the Law is administered. Separated from politics, with income assured and absolutely unassailable, and in a social position of rank by all classes respectfully recognized, a seat on the "Bench" is considered one of the highest honours obtainable in the Dominion.

The Parks of Toronto have so far not had much done to beautify or embellish their natural advantages. *The Riverside Park* is situate upon the banks of the Don at the eastern limits of the City. Upon the shores of the Humber Bay, at the west end, and adjoining the windings of the Humber River, is "*The High Park.*" Extending over an area of four hundred acres it comprises within its boundaries great possibilities for landscape gardening. Roads have been opened through its winding dells and rolling hills, skirting the miniature lakes, and opening vistas of distant views, making a drive through its woodland glades a pleasurable outing. Pic-nickers revel in its groves, and steamboats and railway trains give hourly access.

The Queen's Park of about fifty acres in extent, is situated in the heart of the City, and is approached through THE COLLEGE AVENUE, 120 feet wide and a mile in length, bordered on either side by horse chestnuts and elms. On gaining the Park the road passes the *Russian guns* captured by the British troops at Sebastopol, and presented by the British Government to the city.

THE COLLEGE AVENUE.

The bands of the volunteer regiments play here on Saturday evenings during the summer from the band stand under the trees.

The drive then sweeps along the edge of a ravine to the *Volunteers' Monument*, erected in memory of those who fell during the Fenian raid, in 1866. On the summit—Britannia. Below—Two Infantry Volunteers, and emblematical figures of Hope and Grief. An effective railing of crossed rifles surmounts the base.

Opposite to this is the bronze statue of the *Hon. George Brown* one of the foremost Canadian politicians of his day, and the founder of the *Globe* newspaper. The figure, which is of heroic size, represents the orator in the act of speaking, and is a very effective work of art. The sculptor was C. B. Burch, A.R.A., London, Eng. The Park is well wooded with old forest trees, principally oaks, and has much natural beauty. Surrounding it are many villa residences. The road winds down a hill and passing a small sheet of water next comes in view upon the opposite slope.

The University of Toronto.—This noble Norman Gothic group of buildings is the finest example of its style of architecture in America —whether in its massive proportions or in the mediæval detail of the carvings in stone, no two of which are the same.

The principal front is of great grandeur, a massive tower rises in the centre flanked by wings on either side with long ranges of varied windows ; to the left a picturesque minaret with shady cloister below, and a circular building containing the *Laboratory*.

UNIVERSITY OF TORONTO.

The whole group forms three sides of a square, with an internal quadrangle ; the west wing contains the students' quarters, and the east wing with the Octagon Tower and Convocation Hall is one of the most excellent portions of the design.

On the *Entrance Doorway* are the Arms of the College, and columns of richly carved stone. The entrance hall and long corridors ead to *The Convocation Hall*, with high gabled oak roof, carved in grotesque forms. The stained glass triple window is in memory of the Students who fell defending the frontier in 1866. On the *Senate Stairway* are some marvellous carvings in white Caën stone of Canadian birds. These, as works of the highest merit, should not be missed. The *Library*, a splendid chamber, with inviting quiet recesses, contains 40,000 volumes, also a statue of William of Wykeham. The *Museum* contains a collection of birds, beasts and curiosities, well worthy of a visit. A winding stair, of 160 steps from this level, leads to the top of the *Tower*, from whence a fine view of Toronto and its environs is obtainable, and on clear days, of the cloud of spray hovering over the Niagara Falls. The keys must be obtained from the curator. The details of the designs and of the carvings in stone of this building are worthy of close study, as having been framed on the best examples of European architecture. It will be noticed that there is no repetition. Every column and capital is a separate study, and each enrichment a new design. This is applicable to the exterior as well as the interior, and some fantastic Gothic carvings are to be seen about the west cloister and around the eave of the laboratory.

Entrance free, from 10 a.m. to 4 p.m.

Big Tom, whose solemn tones are to be heard from the tower at 9 o'clock every evening, when the students are in residence, weighs

On the opposite side of the lawn is the Tower and Dome of the *Observatory*, now the home of the Meteorological Department for the Dominion, or what is more popularly known as, "Old Probabilities." From here the daily weather forecasts are telegraphed to all parts of the Dominion. Every mail train starting in the morning, in all parts of Canada, carries on its mail car a large signal which can be seen as it passes along, and indicates the weather for the day. Thus the country as well as the town's people get the advantage of the forecasts. This establishment was originally initiated by the British Government some thirty years ago, and during that time and now meteorological observations are made and recorded by skilled observers, every minute without intermission! a quiet, unostentatious pursuit of scientific knowledge, which few are aware goes on in their midst.

The monstrosity in red brick alongside, is the *School of Technology*.

McMaster College, the training college for the Baptist clergy, is at the head of the Queen's Park. This was founded and endowed by the Hon. Wm. McMaster, a wealthy resident of Toronto, and its handsome Credit Valley stone facade forms a very effective grouping in the midst of the surrounding trees.

KNOX COLLEGE—TORONTO.

Further to the West of the Park is KNOX COLLEGE, well situated at the head of Spadina Avenue. This is the headquarters of the educational work of the Presbyterian Church of Canada. The College was formed in 1844, and is well endowed. The present buildings were erected in 1875, and are occupied by six professors and about one hundred students.

On the east side of the Queen's Park is *St. Michael's College*, occupying an excellent position on the crown of Clover Hill. Here is carried on the higher education of the Roman Catholic body of the Province of Ontario. Close by it is the excellent young ladies' school, kept in *St. Mary's Convent* by the nuns of the order.

TRINITY COLLEGE.

In the west end of the city, and standing in its own grounds, TRINITY COLLEGE, built in the early English style, has a quaint scholastic air. The facade is pleasantly diversified with cut stone dressings and projecting bay windows, while the bell turrets above (yclept by the students "pepper pots") add much to the appearance.

The newly added *Chapel*, whose plain exterior rather mars the continuity of the facade, is admirably finished and arranged in its interior, and is worthy of inspection.

The *Convocation Hall* has a handsome oak roof highly carved, and portraits of founders and chancellors of the University.

The students' quarters are in the wings. The College is the seat of the Anglican or Episcopal Church in Canada under a Royal charter, and was erected by the exertions of Bishop Strachan in 1851. It has an outlying branch in "Trinity School," at Port Hope, a boys' school of rare excellence, and founded and conducted on the lines of the great English public schools.

The *University of Trinity College* and the *University of Toronto* are the only corporations having power to confer degrees, the other colleges being colleges of instruction "in affiliation." It will be readily seen that Toronto is thus quite a "University City," and when during the winter the Colleges are in session there are fully 1,500 students in residence.

In addition to these, the *Toronto Veterinary College*, numbering on an average 300 students, has a Continental reputation, and some first-class *Business Colleges* are also in operation.

On the western limits of the city, upon the shores of the beautiful curve of the Humber Bay, is the *High Park*, comprising 400 acres of hill and dale of varied wood-land seenery. The Humber River affords pleasant boating jaunts, and the views over the lake, from the high lands in the rear, are well worth the drive.

In *Parkdale* will be found *The Home for Incurables*, one of the most perfectly conducted charities of the city. Visitors are cordially welcomed. The view from the top of the central tower gives a better idea of the geographical location of the city than is obtainable from any other place, and is worth seeing.

The Exhibition Buildings, most prominently set on the Lake shore, are complete in every respect, and at the time of the Fall Fairs in September are thronged with visitors from all parts. The grounds are open and maintained by the city as a park, with flower gardens in the summer, making a pleasant and cool drive.

The Central Prison for men, and the *Mercer Reformatory* or Prison for women, are open to visitors upon orders from the Government Inspector of Prisons. In the *Provincial Lunatic Asylum*, with large central dome and wide extending wings, are collected the insane from all parts of Ontario.

At the intersection of King and Simcoe streets are *Upper Canada College*, the oldest boys' school in the Province, and *St. Andrew's*

Church, a splendid edifice in the old Scotch baronial style, of massive stone-work and arched windows, the abode of the "Old Kirk." GOVERNMENT HOUSE, the palatial residence of the Lieutenant-

Governor of Ontario, is on the opposite corner. The valley which winds through the gardens is the last reminiscence of "Russell's Creek," up which Governor Simcoe used to row from the Bay when he first chose Toronto to be his capital. The gardens are well kept, and the conservatories well stocked. In the interior is a very handsome main entrance hall, with grand staircase; to the left is the suite of Presence Chambers, in which the receptions and levees are held. Beyond these are the conservatories and ball-room. In the dining-room is a fine collection of life-size portraits of the Governors of Upper Canada from its cession to the British Crown. Permission to view the interior must be obtained by letter from the *A.D.C. in waiting.*

POST-OFFICE.

There are many other fine buildings; among them THE POST-OFFICE, and the many surrounding Financial Institutions upon Toronto street, which is fast becoming the Lombard or Wall street of Toronto.

Upon King street will have been noticed a fine building bearing the title, "Manning's Arcade;" passing through the archway in its centre, access is gained to THE GRAND OPERA HOUSE. The interior is of good form, and has a seating capacity of 2,300, with a large and spacious stage adapted to the production of the most exacting plays. The traditions of the house include reminiscences of the best modern actors—Fechter, Irving, Booth, Boucicault, Neilson, Bernhardt, and others. Toronto audiences are proverbially of high requirements and acute taste—no doubt in great degree from the large and educated student population, whose approval and

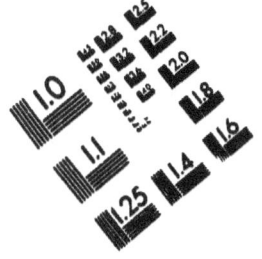 

**IMAGE EVALUATION
TEST TARGET (MT-3)**

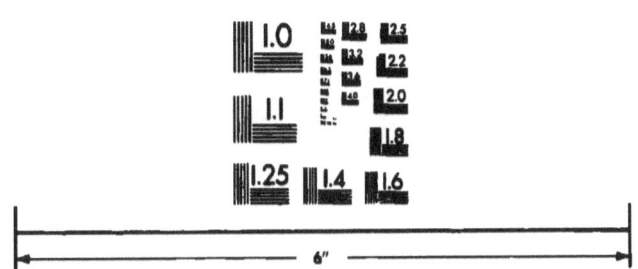

Photographic
Sciences
Corporation

23 WEST MAIN STREET
WEBSTER, N.Y. 14580
(716) 872-4503

GRAND OPERA HOUSE.

disapproval of the plays submitted to its criticism is frequently expressed in unmistakeable terms. This healthy expression of mercurial temperament—pulsating with the progress of the action on the stage—is of like character with that found at the theatres in Dublin; and thus it is that not a few companies—the fascinating Adelaide Neilson's among them—have preferred to submit new plays to the audiences at "the Grand" before bringing them to the less exacting and more coldly undemonstrative audiences of the United States.

In the outskirts of the city are many pleasant drives : *The Valley of the Don, Todmorden, Norway, Davenport,* etc., while the Summer afternoon water excursions by steamers to *Niagara, Victoria Park, Scarboro' Heights, Humber Bay, Mimico, Oakville, Hamilton,* etc., at fares from 25 cents to $1.00, serve to diversify the visitor's stay. Situated as Toronto is, upon the shores of Lake Ontario, the summer heats are tempered by the presence of the broad expanse of water and attendant breezes; whatever may have been the heat of the day, it rarely ever extends into the night, so after sundown the cool air and soft summer evenings make the city—what it really is—a pleasant lake-side resort.

Off for a Real Good Fish.

GENTLEMAN (to grocer)—" Two gallons Santa Cruz, one gallon Old Tom, two gallons Maryland Club, four dozen Pommery Sec, four dozen Milwaukee and six boxes of Reina Vics."
GROCER—" Yes, sir. That all, sir ?"
GENTLEMAN—" Er— Do you keep fishing tackle ?"
GROCER—" Yes, sir, full line, sir."
GENTLEMAN—" Ah—Put in a couple of fish hooks."

The Northern Lakes.

Our tourists will now direct their attention to the trip to the " Interior," and the country stretching 200 miles northward of Toronto, towards the Georgian Bay and the Inland Lakes. Until recently it was a wilderness, but within twenty years or so numerous towns and hamlets have sprung up; many summer hotels have been opened at attractive points, and settlers have poured in with a rapidity equal to the settlement of many parts of the Western States. Railroads have penetrated into its heart. Steamboats ply upon its larger lakes, and some excellent highways traverse its length and breadth. It is emphatically a country of forests, lakes, and rivers. The lakes vary greatly in size, the larger ones thirty and forty miles in length, and the smaller ones mere ponds, but clear and deep, and all abounding in salmon-trout, perch, black-bass and speckled trout.

THE NORTHERN AND NORTH-WESTERN RAILWAY

Is one of the connecting links between the frontier and the interior. Leaving Toronto by one of the express trains furnished with fine parlour cars, the passengers will pass through a populous and rich country, with substantial farm houses and extensive saw-mills at intervals, along the whole line. The appointments of the railway are first-class, and the station houses, models of neatness and beauty, have tasteful flower gardens and lawns attached, with jets of water spurting from fountains that cool and refresh the plants.

At *Parkdale* will be noticed the *Subway*, by which Queen street, the great east and west artery of the city, passes under the converging railways. At this point the Canadian Pacific, Grand Trunk and Northern Railways all enter the city. The growth of the suburbs shows itself along the next couple of miles, where the houses are gradually creeping farther and farther into the country and streets of buildings occupy the receding farms.

At four miles is *Davenport*, a hill side locality fast filling with suburban residences, having a pretty station, with flower-garden and high-gabled roof.

On the left between this station and Weston, is seen the Valley of the Humber River and the heights of the Caledon Hills which close the distant view to the west. Toward the south will be seen the blue outline of the lake with the wooded points about Mimico jutting out into its waters.

The height of land between Lakes Ontario and Huron, which is reached at twenty-six miles from Toronto, is 755 feet above the level of Lake Ontario, and 415 feet above that of Lake Huron.

A few miles beyond King the line passes by not a few curves through " The Ridges." Here, within the confines of a single farm, the waters diverge on either side the summit of the water-shed. One streamlet running south forms the tiny headwaters of the infant *Humber*, whose mouth debouches into Lake Ontario at Toronto, the other winds its way northward to the Holland River on its way to the Georgian Bay, and thence returns by Lake Erie and over the Niagara Falls to reunite their waters in Lake Ontario, after a circuit of over 800 miles.

The train emerges from the turnings among the hills and on the left is caught a pleasant view over the finely nurtured farms of the " *Vale of Aurora*." The hill-sides dotted with comfortable farm steadings, the rounded copses of hardwood trees and the spires of the little village churches give a picture which might be taken out of fair England itself.

"*Glen Lonely*" the ancestral home of the descendants of the Chevalier de St. George, "*Larchmere*" of the Baldwins and "*Elmwoods*" the country house and stock farm of W. Mulock, Esq., the Member for the County, are among the favourite holdings in this favoured Vale, which has a well-earned renown for the excellence of its horses and its sheep.

Next is *Newmarket*, the county town of the County of York, with a population of 5,000. A place of considerable age and importance, and the headquarters of some energetic manufacturing interests.

The corner-stone of the picturesque church on the hill-side to the left, was laid by His Excellency Lord Dufferin, during his progress in 1874.

In a little while a small stream will be noticed on the right, meandering sometimes through grassy meadows and again through groves of forest elms. It is the first gathering of the Holland River and the first water on which used to be shipped the canoes of the Indians and of the voyageurs, in times long past, after they had passed over the carrying place or "portage" from the harbour at Toronto.

By it came the fierce invading Iroquois when they made their too successful incursions and decimated the tribes of the Hurons that lived between the banks of Lake Simcoe and the shores of the Georgian Bay. Along this valley, too, were carried the munitions of war and the materials for the equipment of the naval squadron and the Navy-yard, which, in the early years of the country, was maintained at Penetanguishene.

Holland Landing, now a quiet and picturesque village, was the point at which the heavy goods were transferred to the large batteaux for transport across Lake Simcoe. Its pretty white church, with square tower stands on the hill-side to the right, and long ago looked down upon a busy scene, when all the business of the North passed on long lines of heavy laden waggons before its doors. Sir John Franklin called here when on his first expedition overland to the North Pole in 1825, and in 1827 Galt passed by on his way to Goderich, *via* Penetanguishene.

Near by, on the village green rests a gigantic anchor, which having come all the way over the sea from Her Majesty's dockyards, in England, and by the laborious work of sixteen yoke of oxen, been hauled thus far on its way to the "Navy Yard," was interrupted on its

THE ANCHOR AT HOLLAND LANDING.

journey by the declaration of peace, and now remains to form a quaint monument and record of the early days of the Great Portage.

Bradford (42 miles) is at the crossing of the river and close to the *Holland River Marsh*, a locality celebrated among sportsmen for its abundant supply of partridge, snipe, wild duck and hares. There is good trolling in the river for maskinonge. First-class accommodation can be got at Bingham's Hotel, Bradford, and information respecting guides, punts, etc.

LAKE SIMCOE.

At *Lefroy* is seen the first view of *Lake Simcoe*, the first of the various chains of inland lakes which are now met with in succession. Stages run regularly to *Belle Ewart*, 1½ miles on the shore of the Lake, here called Cook's Bay. A name given by Lieutenant-Governor Simcoe, after Captain Cook, the great circumnavigator of the globe, who had been master of the ship "Pembroke," on which the Lieut.-Governor's father was captain during the expedition against Quebec, in 1759; Major Holland, after whom the river was named, also served in the same conquest.

A ferry steamer keeps up constant connection with *Roach's Point*, whose houses can be seen on the opposite shore of the Bay. This pretty village is much frequented by tourists in summer on account of its nearness to Toronto and excellent boating and fishing—bass, trout and maskinonge—Raike's Hotel and several family boarding-houses.

Serpent Island will be seen on the lake, where linger a few remnants of the Huron tribe who even still continue to make pilgrimages to join their brethren on the *Christian Islands* at their annual tribal gatherings.

Allandale is the junction point of the Northern and North-Western Railway system. Here join together from the south the North-Western Branch from Hamilton and the Northern Branch from Toronto. Three lines radiate north.

The Muskoka Branch to the Lakes of Muskoka, Callandar, the Canadian Pacific and the all rail route round the north shores of Lake Superior.

The Penetanguishene Branch to Midland, Matchedash and Penetang Bays, and the Parry Island Archipelago (42 miles).

The Collingwood Branch to Collingwood, on the shores of the Georgian Bay, where connection is made with the splendid steamers of the "Collingwood Lake Superior Line," for the grand tour of Lake Superior, Thunder Bay, Silver Islet, Nipegon, etc., the water route to the North-West, *via* Port Arthur and Duluth and Georgian Bay Line the Great Northern Transit Co. for Manitoulin Islands, the Great North Channel, Mackinac, Sault Ste. Marie, Parry Sound, etc. An excellent refreshment station is maintained at this junction, and trains stop for meals. The monument in the garden was erected by the men of the railway to the memory of Col. Fred. W. Cumberland, who for twenty-two years was General Manager of the Company. During that time he had succeeded in conducting the railway to the satisfaction of the people whom it served and in winning the personal attachment of every man in his employ. The Bronze is an excellent likeness—the work of a Canadian artist, Mr. F. Dunbar.

The arm of Lake Simcoe on which the station stands, is *Kempenfeldt Bay*, named after another naval hero, whose loss with all his crew v the sinking of the *Royal George*, when lying at anchor in h. .our at Spithead, sent a thrill throughout the world.

> His sword was in its sheath,
> His fingers held the pen,
> When Kempenfeldt when down,
> With twice four hundred men.
>
> —COWPER.

Barrie, the county town of the County of Simcoe, is a prosperous place of 5,000 inhabitants. Its houses and church spires rising picturesquely upon the sloping hill sides, are seen on the opposite shores of the bay, around the head of which the railway comes. Barrie is a delightful summer resort, with an excellent fleet of boats and yachts, some of which will be seen lying at their anchorages; and there are some good fishing streams in the neighbourhood.

The steamer connects from Barrie with the new summer hotel at *Big Bay Point*, nine miles down the Kempenfeldt Bay, where it joins with the main water of the lake and forms a splendid place for

THE NORTHERN LAKES OF CANADA.

excursion parties, for whom very favourable rates are made (*see adv.*) Apply to Isaac Robinson, Allandale.

In passing down the bay some admirably situated private residences will be seen on both shores at *Shanty Bay* on the north, and *Strath Allan* on the south.

The main water being entered, Lake Simcoe is one of the largest inland Lakes of Ontario, being 30 miles long and 16 miles broad. Its shores are characterized by great sylvan beauty.

At *Keswick* may be seen the charmingly situated resort of one of the great lumber kings of the country, and many of the other choice spots begin to be occupied with the summer residences of the more wealthy inhabitants.

Serpent Island, Lighthouse, and other islands are at the south end.

Sutton is pleasantly situated upon a sheltered bay on the south shore of the lake, and is the terminus of the Nipissing Branch of the G. T. Railway.

The steamer then skirts the upper shores of the lake, past deep bays, whose wooded promontories jut out picturesquely into the lake, and sighting *Atherly*, after an easy run of two hours, passes *Grape* and other islands closely clustered together, and enters the "Narrows," the water channel joining Lake Simcoe with Lake Couchiching, of which the first view is here gained, and passing through the swing bridges of the Muskoka and Midland Railways, soon, upon a point stretching out into the lake, is seen the Couchiching Park. The steamer rounds the point, and our "water tourist" is landed at Orillia.

Continuing on by rail from Barrie, the train skirts the shores of Lake Simcoe and pleasant vistas of its waters are gained.

Near *Hawkstone* are some excellent speckled trout streams.

The train plunges into an almost continuous line of forest and, emerging once more on the shore of the lake, a view is seen (to the right) of *Grape Island* and the others grouped together at the head of Lake Simcoe.

The rails curve across the neck of land between the lakes and reach *Orillia*. Fast rising in importance, the town is situated at the foot of Lake Couchiching upon a hill side facing the water. It is a favourite centre of summer travel, the hotels excellent and the neighbourhood enjoyable. Close by is the beautiful *Couchiching Park* and the neighbourhood gives scope for pleasant rides and drives, while sailing and boating, and the steamers " Orillia," Cariella," etc., on Lakes Simcoe and Couchiching, afford opportunities for

GRAPE ISLAND—LAKE SIMCOE.

charming water parties and picnics, A pretty trip of fifteen miles is made by the steamer Orillia through the Narrows to *Strawberry Island*, situated at the head of Lake Simcoe. It is forty five acres in extent, partially cleared and partially wooded. *Strawberry Island Hotel* is an excellent summer resort with fine sandy beach for bathing (*see advt.*), good boating and camping. The fishing for black bass in the neighbourhood is renowned, particularly at *Starvation Island*, whose fame is well known among adepts. Capt. C. McInnes, Orillia, will answer all questions.

Among other points of interest on the lakes to the visitor from Orillia are the Ojibbeway settlement of Indians at Rama, Chief Island, Longford, the Quarries, the Rapids and Falls of the Severn, and Washago, at the head of Lake Couchiching.

LAKE COUCHICHING.

Couchiching ! Well may the curious tourist, struck by the peculiarity of the name, ask its meaning. Indian nomenclature is always appropriate and descriptive ; here the varying breezes, welcome adjuncts of a summer resort, that fan the surface of the lake, have given the Indian name for " Lake of many winds." This locality is among the highest in Ontario, being 750 feet above Lake Ontario, 415 above Lake Huron, and 390 feet above Lake Superior ; and it is the next lake to Lake Simcoe in the chain that empty their waters by the River Severn into the Georgian Bay and Lake Huron.

The rapidity of the rise from Lake Ontario may thus be judged ; and the consequent elevation and clearness of the atmosphere, and the cool breezes, would, apart from any other consideration, be sufficient to commend the locality as a favourite one for a summer visit.

The black bass, pickerel, and salmon-trout fishing in the lake is most excellent ; and ready access is gained, from Orillia as a central point, to the celebrated Sparrow Lake, where maskinonge, black bass, speckled-trout, etc., are found in abundance, and the best of duck and partridge shooting in season.

The Midland Railway here connects with the Georgian Bay ; and excursions may be made to Midland, Penetanguishene, Parry Sound, and to the island district of the lake, and to the trout streams of the rivers Coldwater and Severn.

There are a number of summer residences of Canadian citizens around the shores, and the visitor from a distance should not fail to " lay off " at Orillia, so that he may thus get a full idea of the different chains of lakes, which present marked differences.

A pleasant place is the *Couchiching Park*, situated on the point of a narrow promontory projecting a mile and a half northward into the lake, and surrounded on three sides by water ; thus, come from whatever quarter it may, every breeze has play, while the lake on the one side or the other, being protected by the point from wind and wave, pleasure-boating in safe calm waters can at all times be enjoyed.

Drives and shady walks bordering the margins of the lake are tastefully laid out in a park of 180 acres ; and a handsome avenue, three-fourths of a mile in length, winding through forest trees, leads to the stations of the Northern and Midland Railways. Arbours, erected at convenient places on the lake, extend out into the water, where, sheltered from the sun, the views can be enjoyed. A lovelier

VIEW AT COUCHICHING.

sight could not be wished for. From any portion of the buildings, no matter in what direction you look, fine stretches of water, verdure-clad banks sloping to the water's edge, and green forest glades, present themselves to the eye. Across the bay, in an attractive cove, backed by hills clad to their summits with fresh foliage, lies the now prosperous town of Orillia. To the north, scarcely discernible between the miniature islands that bestud the lake's surface, may be seen the settlement of Ojibbeway Indians, appropriately called Rama, its tin-tipped church spire like a bar of silver under the light of the rising sun, or as a streak of gold under the sunset's declining rays.

At Rama is the "reservation" of the last remnants of the great tribe of the Ojibbeway. Near Longford have been carefully preserved some ancient Indian inscriptions, representing one of the early strifes between this tribe and the Iroquois. The figures of men fighting with spears and bows are roughly scratched upon the lithographic stone, and some traces of colour still remain. At one time all this surrounding land was occupied by their numerous villages, a population of at least 25,000 being settled around the shores of Lakes Simcoe and Couchiching; and now but a few survivors remain, seeming, from their shy and distant manner, almost shrinkingly to excuse themselves for still remaining with us.

In "Tecumseh"—that new and thrilling poem which should be in every Canadian's hand—graphically rises the prophetic lament of *Iena*, the Indian maiden:—

>"Oh, it is pitiful to creep in fear
>O'er lands where once our fathers stept in pride!
>The Long-Knife strengthens, while our race decays,
>And falls before him as our forests fall.
>His flowers, his very weeds, displace our own—
>Agressive as himself. All, all thrust back!
>Destruction follows us, and swift decay.
>. . . . .
>As clouds will sheer small fleeces from their sides,
>Which, melting in our sight as in a dream,
>Will vanish all like phantoms in the sky.
>So melts our heedless race!
>—MAIR.

In the Park, or around the shores, bathing-houses, dancing platforms, bowling-alleys, croquet lawns, and cricket grounds, afford every means of amusement.

It is but a short row by water, or ride by land, from Orillia, so that the Couchiching Park is one of the additional advantages for summer stay at this town.

Splendid brook trout are caught in the streams in the neighbourhood, and the finest black bass fishing in America is in these surrounding lakes. (*See Hallock's Sportsman's Gazetteer.*)

The tourist having "stopped over" either at Orillia or Couchiching is again given choice of two routes, either by "water" on steamer up Lake Couchiching (14 miles), calling at the different little ports, to *Washago* where the train is again taken: or by "all rail" by the Northern Railway. After crossing the Narrows swing bridge, the line passes through forests, through which distant views are obtained of Lake Couchiching to the left and Lake St. John to the right. At *Longford* is a large lumbering establishment, and after *Washago*, where the water tourists join the train, is the village of *Severn Bridge*. The place takes its name from the noble stream, the Severn, which runs westward throughout, draining the whole area of its great tributary the *The Black River* and of Lake Simcoe into the Georgian Bay.

SEVERN RAPIDS—SPARROW LAKE.

SPARROW LAKE.

First among the sporting districts of the Northern Lakes, met on the northward trip, is the Severn River. At Severn Bridge the tourist will take boat or steamer, and after a short run down the River Severn, reach

Sparrow Lake has long been celebrated for the excellence of its fishing, but particularly for the deer, duck and ruffled grouse shooting obtainable in their proper seasons. Many spots are available for pic-nics and camping, especially near the rapids at the lower end. Proceeding further down the river, an interesting canoe route is available, and easily traced through Beaver, Legs and Pine Lakes, with short portages to Gravenhurst, for which Indians and canoes can be got at Rama. An easy one day excursion to Sparrow Lake and return can be made from Orillia.

Proceeding down the Severn River, a splendid fishing trip can be made following the stream through Six-Mile Bay and Gloucester Pool to its outlet in Georgian Bay, opposite Waubaushene and Penetanguishene. There are many portages and difficult rapids. The trip should, therefore, not be attempted without guides. Canoe and guide will cost about $2.00 per day. These can be obtained at Rama or Orillia. The Severn is the line of division between the frontier counties and of the Free Grant district of Muskoka, which is here entered. Having crossed the river upon a lofty bridge, the line passes the height of land separating the Lakes of Muskoka from Lake Couchiching. False impressions of the free grant district are frequently taken from the appearance of the country seen along this part of the trip; but, as on the south side there are tracts of fine farming land, so, to the north, this ridge being passed over, lies the wide arable country which is being so rapidly peopled by thrifty settlers.

The *Kasheshebogamog*, a small stream with a very long name, is a few miles afterwards crossed. This awful word is usually observed to have such a knock-down effect upon strangers that they subside into a gentle melancholy for the rest of the trip, apparently lost in wonder at the ingenuity which could invent so big a name for so small a river. Some folks of extra powers of mind have been known to enquire the name of the next creek, but such cases are few and far between.

It may have been noticed that south of Washago, being the country adjacent to the Lake Simcoe Chain of Lakes, all the rocks are of limestone formations. After passing the Severn nothing but granite meets the eye; massive in form, deep red in colour, and with a micaseous sheen shining through it.

As we wind through the "divide" the granite rocks raise high their lofty sides, bluff cliffs overhang the railway as it curves around their

bases, in some places the front portion of the Train is lost to sight from the rear, but finally the "Granite Notch" is reached, and the railway slips through a natural gap, fortunately left for its passage by nature.

At twenty-seven miles from Orillia (115 from Toronto) is *Gravenhurst*, a rising village at the foot of the chain of the "*Lakes of Muskoka*," and the point of transfer to the steamer for this, the second chain of lakes.

From Niagara Falls via Hamilton.

In addition to the route by the Niagara River, Lake Ontario and Toronto, access to these inland lakes is gained *via* Hamilton. The Grand Trunk Railway from Suspension Bridge passes through a beautiful country, well cultivated, and full of orchards, which line the fore-shore at the foot of the high elevation which follows the lake, and at the foot of which the railway runs.

Near *Merritton* the railway passes under the Welland Canal, by a short tunnel, and a passing glimpse is got of the magnificent new locks of the New Welland Canal and of the smaller and more picturesque locks and weir-gates, with miniature water-falls of the Old canal.

St. Catharines, the Sanatarium of Western Canada, and whose health-restoring waters have a world-wide reputation, is seen to the right on the farther side of the valley through which the old Welland Canal finds its way to the waters of Lake Ontario, and soon the lake itself comes into view. At the foot of its "Mountain" nestles

THE CITY OF HAMILTON.

Transfer is here made from the Grand Trunk to the station of the Northern and North-Western R. R., the only line whose trains run to the Lakes of Muskoka.

The city is built upon one of the steps or terraces which surround the lake, and would appear to have at one time formed the immediate shore. Looking down from the elevation of the "Mountain," its streets slope away towards the lake and diminish in the distant perspective. The form of the harbour, closed in from the open water by the Burlington Beach, is clearly limned, and away to the left stretches the pretty valley in the midst of which can be seen the spires and chimnies of the little town of Dundas.

Before Hamilton was Dundas had been. At this latter place, as being the head of navigation, which by means of the Burlington Canal was extended to its very doors, in early days had been concentrated the busy commerce of all the country west. To this place came for shipment to the sea all the golden grain, and back from it

HAMILTON FROM THE MOUNTAIN.

trailed the heavy waggons laden with the merchandise purchased in exchange. But times have changed. The construction the of Great Western Railway altered the course of business and the young rival, Hamilton, has grown into the dimensions of a city of the first-rating, while decorous seemly old age has set its placid mark upon the more ancient town.

Hamilton has been fortunate in its inhabitants,—men of nerve, energy and combination. They have, whatever may have been their internal competitions, always pulled together for the weal of their fair city.

Reaching out to bring commerce to their doors, they created the construction of the Great Western, and Wellington Grey and Bruce to the west ; the Northern and North-Western R. R.'s to their north, and the Lake Erie R.R. to the south—and thus their city has become the largest manufacturing centre in Ontario, and its forward progress for ever secured. To-day Hamilton produces one thirty-fourth in value of all the manufactures produced throughout the Dominion, and consumes one-fourteenth of all the coal used in the Province of Ontario.

At the foot of the mountain will be seen the handsome homes of some of its merchant princes. The large building with wide extended wings on the crest of the hill, is the Government Lunatic Asylum. In the centre of the city are the prettily kept gardens of the " Gore of Hamilton," and around it some business edifices which would do credit to any capital. Few better are to be found anywhere than the " Canada Life " and the " Post Office " Buildings.

Dundurn Park, on the heights towards the edge of the bay, is a favourite resort. The Royal Hotel, centrally situated on the main street, is fully recommended.

From Hamilton the connection to the Northern Lakes of Canada is by the North Western R.R.

After running for some distance through the town the railway reaches

BURLINGTON BEACH.

Across the upper end of Lake Ontario, where the shores of the Lake have approached within five miles of one another, the sweeping action of the easterly storms has in long centuries formed a narrow continuous bank or bar of sand, stretching from shore to shore and varying from 600 to 1,000 feet in width. On the east the rollers of Lake Ontario toss their surge ; to the west, protected by it, lie the placid waters of *Burlington Bay*, the harbour of Hamilton. Composed of clear shingly pebbles and pure sharp sand, its five miles length of level continuous beach resembles the sea-shore in its extent, and the distant blue horizon of the great Lake, where the sails of passing vessels fade away and disappear beneath its edge, adds to the illusion. The railway runs along the crown of the bank between the separated waters; a large number of pretty private residences have been erected by the citizens of Hamilton, and near the swing bridge over the canal which has been cut through the bank to join the lake and the harbour, is the pretty Burlington Beach Station. The *Burlington Beach Hotel* is just opposite the station. Its unrivalled situation and fresh and airy surroundings make it a very favourite resort, and visitors from a distance enjoy the fresh breezes together with many of the members of families of Hamilton, whose business does not permit them to go farther away from home.

Bowling alleys and billiard rooms in separate buildings, and a fleet of row boats on the bay side, give plenty of scope for amusement, while for any one who is fond of yachting, there is scarcely a more favourable position on the inland lakes. The yachts of the Hamilton Yacht Club are moored just behind the hotel and excellent sailing craft can be hired for sails down the lake.

The fast iron steamer "Southern Belle" keeps up daily communication between Toronto and Hamilton, calling at Oakville, with its acres of strawberries, and at Burlington Beach each way, giving a pretty coasting trip of thirty-three miles along the shores between the two cities.

THE NORTH-WESTERN RAILWAY.

Having crossed over the Swing Bridge, the railway commences to make its ascent to the upper levels of the interior. High bridges spanning deep gullies are from time to time met with. At *Georgetown* (36 miles) is met the Grand Trunk R.R., by which tourists from Western Canada come, and at *Cardwell Junction*, at the foot of the Caledon Hills, connection is made with the Owen Sound Branch of the Canadian Pacific Railway.

The country passed through exhibits all that could be desired from a farming point of view, particularly near *Beeton*, where the hill sides rolling up in closer profusion, show breadths of grain and pasture that tell of solid agricultural knowledge of high degree, and of the wealth which does not fail to follow it.

At *Beeton* is the centre of the honey interest of Ontario—What was once a pastime has by hard-headed intelligence been brought to be a talented business craft, and the tons of honey marketed at this "Bee town" affect the markets of the whole world. There are regular bee-farms and bee-nurseries. The pedigrees of the hives are as closely watched and cared for as those of herds of cattle, and isolated islands on the Georgian Bay are brought into requisition for the purity and nurture of the parent swarms. All this has brought the honey produce from being only a few years ago a rarity, mainly in the hands of chemists, to be a common article in daily use.

At this point the railway divides into two branches; the one going off by the Blue Mountains and the valley of the Mad River to join the Georgian Bay at Collingwood.

The other by a short run through a pretty country brings the train to the junction station at Allandale.

My Little Girl's First Fish.

My thoughts often travel back to my early fishing days. I cannot remember my first trout or my first bass, or even my own first fish. I imagine this epoch occurred when I wore petticoats and short breeches but I can, and always will remember the first fish of the little girl that calls me papa.

About the time she could talk she began to take an interest in my fishing-tackle, and whenever I brought out the box containing it she was my interested audience. She asked over and over again the name of each particular article the box contained, and was soon able to inform her mother, whom she thought not so well posted, what each article was for.

Early in her little life she administered a rebuke on this subject to her cousin, a little boy, several years her senior. He said:

"Uncle, how many fish-poles have you got?"

Her prompt comment was: "Those are not fish-poles, they are fish-*rods*; you cut poles in the woods."

Many a confidential talk have we had upon the subject of fishing, and more than one promise did she extract from me that when she was a "little bigger girl" I would take her fishing.

One day, taking the baby and nurse out for a drive, I put a hook and line in my pocket. A few miles out we came to a trout stream, and while the carriage stood on the bridge that crossed it, I caught a trout from beneath it. I wish some stern parent, who looks with disfavour upon hooks and lines in the hands of his children, could have seen the eager look in the great blue eyes of that baby while I was waiting for a bite, and the smile that lighted up her little face when I put the trout, alive and struggling, into her fat little hands. Was she afraid of it? Not a bit. Did she let it go? No. She held it tightly with one hand, and with a little finger of the other she pointed out the bright spots, opened its mouth to look down its throat, and examined its eyes and fins. She would not let go of her prize; so I took her home to her mother, smelling strongly of fish, and as well covered with trout slime as one small trout was capable of covering her.

When my little girl was three years old—and that was only a few years ago—she went out for a pleasant day with her mother and father and grand-mother and aunties.

While on the steamer, she reminded me of my many promises, that she should that day fish for the first time. We were no sooner landed than I procured tackle suitable for the hands of such a little "tot," and from the hotel dock she made her maiden effort in the gentle art. Her eagerness and excitement was for some time a bar to her success, and the sun-fish and rock-bass removed the bait from her hook nearly as fast as I could put it on. She wished to bait her own hook, and would take the worms from the can for this purpose, but I persuaded her that I could do it better.

She did not like the idea of fishing with a pole; she wanted a rod, and thought I was very forgetful not to have brought one. At last, with a scream of delight, she landed a rock-bass, about four inches long. She dropped the pole instantly and grasped the struggling fish— her eyes fairly dancing with delight as she informed me, at the top of her voice, "*I've got one! I've got one!*" In an instant she was gone—like a flash—toward the hotel, to show her capture to her mother. She would not let it out of her hands, but held it up to be admired, assuring the people that "*I* caught it, *all alone!*" with a strong accent on the *I*.

Soon she came back, and when I had told her it was a rock-bass, and why it was called a rock-bass, and answered several other "why's," and she had stuck her finger down the throat of the fish and into its eyes, and turned it over and over, examining it thoroughly, she resumed fishing, with the dead fish on the dock behind her.

No more fish for her that day; it took far too much of her time to turn around and see if the one already caught was safe. With all her watchfulness the little bass came to grief, for another little girl, walking along the dock, kicked it into the water. As it fell with a splash in front of her, she gave one glance over her shoulder to see who could have done this unkind thing, and then down she went, prone on her face, with a suddenness that made my heart leap into my throat, and reached out with her little arm to get her much-prized fish. I was at her side in an instant; and the tears welled into her eyes as she told me of the misfortune that had come to her. I rescued the fish, and all that day she did not trust it again out of her hands.

That night, as we were nearing home, and the little tired body was leaning back on the seat, with her eyes half-closed, but the little hands still tightly grasping the fish, her grandmother said to her:

"Beatrice, of all the things that you have seen or done to-day, what did you most enjoy?"

"*Fishing*," was the sententious but emphatic reply.

She had the fish for her breakfast the next morning; and a prouder or more happy little girl it would have been hard to find. When informed by one of her aunties that it was a "sore-eyed bass," she was positive it did not have sore eyes, for she had examined them.

G

It was a rock-bass, "because *papa said so!*" and her faith in the authority she quoted remains unshaken.

The story of a little girl's first fish may find a tender spot in some parental heart ; but, at all events, lots of other little boys and girls will find abundant opportunities in the happy waters of the lakes of Muskoka to angle for and catch their own "first fish."

The Lakes of Muskoka.

The district known as the Muskoka District occupies the "Highlands of Ontario," many of its lakes being over four hundred feet above the level of Lake Superior—the highest lake of the great St. Lawrence system. From it radiate the various lake and river systems of the Province : The French, Maganetewan, Muskoka, and Muskosh Rivers to the west ; the Petewawa and Ottawa to the east, and the Trent system to the south.

In area it comprises a territory equal in size to that of the kingdom of Belgium, or to come nearer home, five times the size of our own Province of Prince Edward Island. Of this area some eight hundred lakes of all sizes, from thirty miles in length to mere ponds, and their river connections occupy no less than one tenth of its surface. The presence of so much water, not in the shape of sodden swamps, but in quick flowing streams and bright deep lakes contributes, no doubt, to the equable temperature, and combines, with the extreme altitude to that brisk exhilarating effect which the clear atmosphere undoubtedly has upon the visitor. Hay fever does not exist among the inhabitants and is greatly mitigated, and after a sufficient stay, entirely cured to strangers.

The waters are of a peculiar deep brown, except in some of the lakes, and when bathing their buoyancy is peculiarly noticeable and better still they do not leave that certain relaxing effect noticed in more southern fresh waters. It is said that as a beverage they are favourable to any ailments of the kidneys.

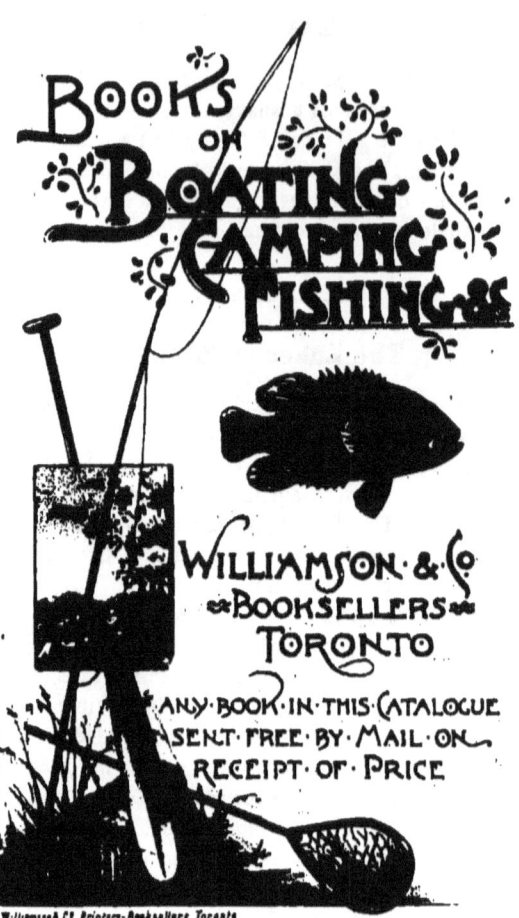

Books on Fishing.
YACHTS—CANOES—CAMPING.

Fishing with the Fly. By C. F. Orvis. Colored plates of 149 standard Salmon, Bass and Trout Flies, with names. $2.75.

Book of the Black Bass. Its scientific and life history, with a treatise on Angling by Dr. Henshall. Fully illustrated. $3.25.

Superior Fishing. Striped Bass, Trout, etc., of North America. By R. P. Rosseveli. Illustrated. $2.25.

The Game Fish of Northern United States and Canada. By R. B. Rossevelt. Illustrated. $2.25.

Fly Rods and Fly Tackle. Suggestions as to the manufacture and use. By H. P. Wells. Illustrated. $3.00.

The Modern Practical Angler. A complete guide to Fly Fishing, Bottom Fishing and Trolling. By H. Prunell. Illustrated. $1.25.

The Book of the Pike. By H. Prunell. Illustrated. $1.25.

The Complete Angler; or, The Contemplative Man's Recreation. By Isaak Walton and Charles Cotton. With six original etchings and two portraits. 450 pp. $10.50.

Fly Fishing. Salmon, Trout and Grayling. By Edward Hamilton, M.D. $2.00.

Frank Forester's Fish and Fishing. Illustrated from nature. By. H. W. Herbert. $2.75.

A Practical Guide to Bottom Fishing, Trowling, Spinning and Fly Fishing. By. J. T. Burgess. With numerous practical illustrations. 50c.

Angling Talks. Being the winter talks on summer pastimes. By George Dawson. 60c.

The Scientific Angler. $1.75.

Sport with Rod and Gun in Canadian and American Woods and Waters. Beautifully illustrated by Alfred M. Mayer. $5.50.

American Sportsman. Containing hints to sportsmen, notes on shooting, etc. By E. J. Lewis, M.D. $3.00.

Williamson & Co.,

The Yacht Sailor. A Treatise on Practical Yachtsmanship, Cruising and Racing. By Vanderdenken. $3.00.

Small Yachts. Their design and construction, exemplified by the ruling types of modern practice, with numerous plates and 70 illustrations, by C. P. Kunhardt. $9.00.

Practical Boat Sailing. With a short vocabulary of nautical terms. By Douglas Frazar. $1.20.

Practical Boat Building. Illustrated. By Kemp. $1.20.

Practical Boat Sailing. By Davis. $2.00

Canoe and Boat Building. A complete manual for amateurs. Containing plans and comprehensive directions for the construction of canoes, rowing and sailing boats, and hunting craft. With numerous illustrations and 24 plates of working drawings, by W. P. Stephens. $1.65.

Canoe Handling. The Canoe—its history, uses, limitations and varieties, practical management and care. Illustrated by C. Bowyer Vaux. $1.25.

Canoeing in Kanuckia; or, Haps and Mishaps Afloat and Ashore. By Norton and Habberton. $1.75.

The Rob Roy on the Baltic. By John Macgregor. $1.25

A Thousand Miles in the Rob Roy Canoe. By John Macgregor. $1.25.

Voyage Alone in the yawl "Rob Roy." By John Macgregor. $1.50.

The Canoe Aurora. A cruise from the Adirondacks to the Gulf. With maps of the route. By Dr. Charles A Neide. $1.25.

Paddle and Portage. $1.50.

Camping and Cruising in Florida. By Dr. Henshall. Illustrated. $1.75.

How to Camp Out. By John M. Gould. $1.00.

Practical Hints on Camping. By H. Henderson. $1.50.

Woodcraft. By Nessmuk. $1.25.

Canoe and Camp Cookery. A practical book for canoeists and others. By Seneca. $1.25.

Camp Life and the Tricks of Trapping. By W. H. Gibson. Illustrated. $1.25.

Booksellers, Toronto.

MAPS & GUIDE BOOKS
—TO—
Famous Fishing Districts

A NEW MAP of Muskoka Lakes, Parry Sound, and Nipissing Districts.
Showing Canoe Routes mentioned in Barlow Cumberland's New Guide to the Northern Lakes. It also shows Railways, Government Roads, Free Grant Lands, and Lumber Limits. In cloth case, convenient for the pocket. *75c.*

MAP AND GUIDE BOOK to the Muskoka Lakes.
Showing all the Islands. By Capt. Rogers, of the Steam Yacht "Sunbeam." Canoeists and Campers will find this an invaluable pocket companion. *50c.*

MUSKOKA, the Picturesque Playground of Canada.
A portfolio of 12 lithographic views (11 x 15) of well-known and picturesque scenes. By Edward Roper. *$1.50.*

A Large Supply of Light Literature for Summer reading always in stock.

WILLIAMSON & CO.
BOOKSELLERS,
No. 5 King Street West, - - Toronto.

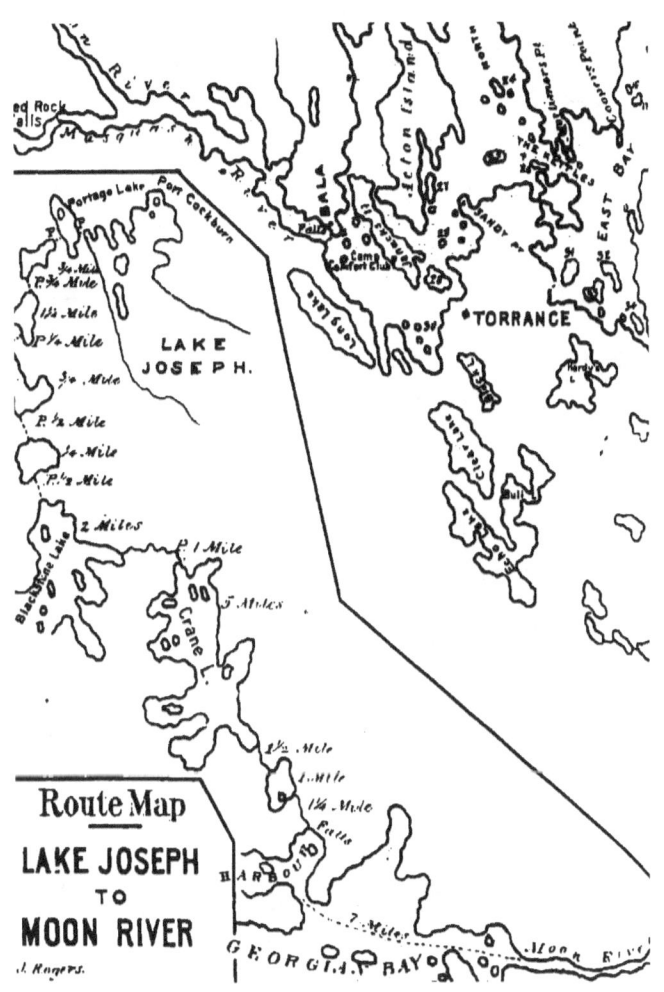

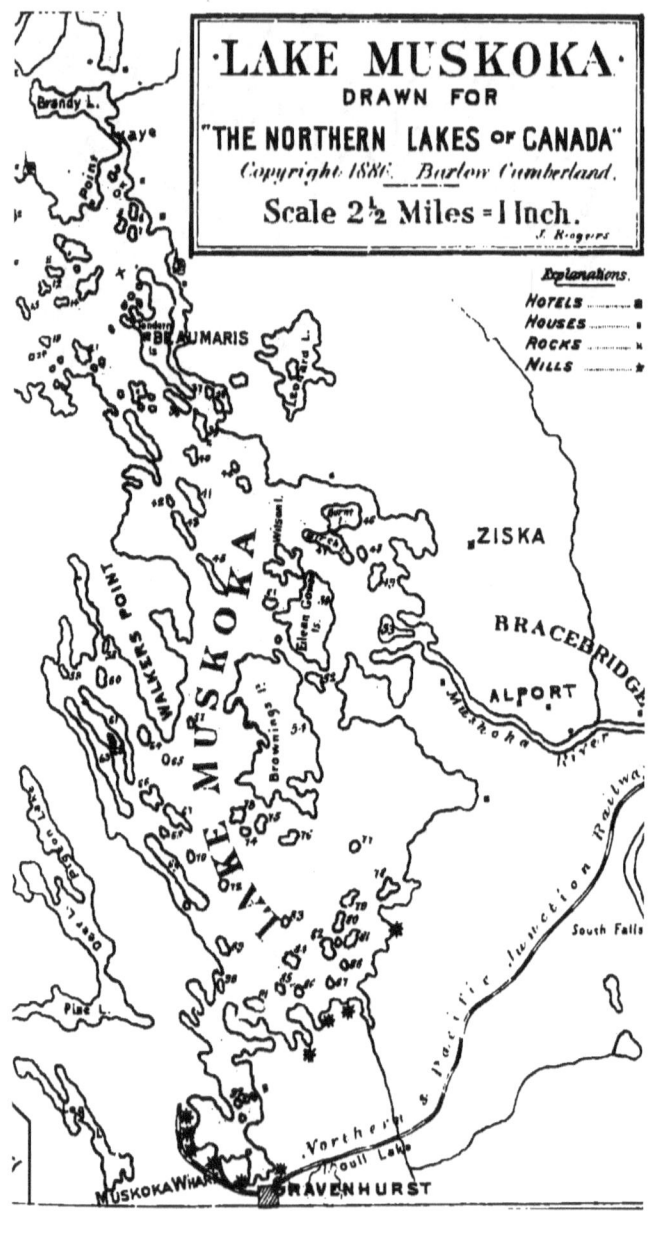

Rocks abound throughout; indeed four-tenths of the country is occupied by rocks and lakes; but both in the water and on the land the rocks jut directly up, so that alongside the base is immediately a good depth of water or of soil. Thus the whole of the remaining sixty per cent. is available for use, and having these adjacent storehouses of moisture or of heat, its powers are largely improved. Grazing is peculiarly successful, and in this branch lies the future of Muskoka. It will become the dairy and the sheep grazing district of the Province, for the rocks of Muskoka seem to have the faculty of nur-

LAKE MUSKOKA.

turing trees, shrubs, and verdure which cling to and cover their sides in a most incomprehensible manner.

The flora of the district is, as might be expected from its situation, peculiar to itself, and walks through the woods will bring to the untaught eye many unaccustomed varieties and to the educated botanist, a rare storehouse of pleasure. One of them says : " The vegetation is almost tropical in its undisturbed luxuriance. The beautiful white fringed Orchis—the loveliest of all the Habenarias—and the splendid Cinnamon and Royal Osmund ferns grow to perfection in low and moist situations, while the Polypody and the Shield-fern flourish in the higher grounds. In the district are also found, in exceptional abundance, Club-mosses of various species, and the curious Pitcher plant nestles in its moss-setting along the margins of the sequestered pools."

The district was long occupied by the various sub-tribes of the Hurons, as being a safe asylum from the fury of the warring nations who occupied the shores of Lake Ontario, while its woods and waters afforded them ample sustenance of fish and game.

The tract is shown upon the *Carte de la Nouvelle France* (Map of New France), published by the early voyageurs and Jesuit Fathers, as lying between the country of the " *Ancien Pays des Hurons*" (Ancient Land of the Hurons) *who were destroyed and scattered by the Iroquois in 1649*), and the country of the "*Pays Outaouais*" (Ottawa tribes). Lake Muskoka was then called by the French "*Petit Lac des Hurons*," and Lake Simcoe "*Lac Toronto.*"

The origin of the name is, as is the case with all names originating from Indian sources, couched in mystery and subject of different opinions. Some assert it is derived from the Indian word " Musquo-tah," signifying " red ground," probably owing to its rusty iron and ochre-coloured sediments which may be seen in the soils of many of the fields, and around the banks of some of the streamlets. Others that its meaning is that of the " Clear-sky-land," a signification which would appear to have some reasonable accuracy, but whatever its meaning may be, we may fairly accept the earliest testimony, and join with Mr. Alex. Sheriff, who in his topographical notices, published by the Quebec Historical Society, in 1831, says: " This river is called the Muskoka, after the Missasaga chief, who used to hunt in some part of its neighbourhood."

This chief's name is elsewhere spelt " Mesqua-Okee." All Indian names have some attendant meaning ; be this whatever it may, it was borne by a gallant warrior and a bold hunter, whose renown spread through the surrounding country. The home of his tribe was hard by the shores of Lake Ontario, and little was it supposed, when he sought sport and recreation in this inland paradise of game, that he was leading the way for so many others to follow exactly in his footsteps, in our later and modern days. Thus we connect the present beautiful and improving district with the romantic and receding past.

Perhaps some of the writers, to whom Canada is now giving birth, will do for this territory what Fenimore Cooper did for those farther south, or Bulwer Lytton has done for Pompeii, and will re-people these ancient homes with the romance and story of their earlier Indian and French occupation. Once more then shall the birch bark canoe, with its dusky occupants, steal through the waters between the silent islands, either in peaceful summer-bright journey, or on expedition of deadly internecine hate.

Gravenhurst. This town, now grown to considerable estate, has been always the Gateway to the Muskoka district. Here used to arrive the wearied stages after their fourteen miles jolting over the rocks and through the gullies which line the whole way over the portage from *Washago,* where the last transfer was made from the steamers. How many a heart has sank in despair as the forbidding rocks seemed almost to crowd out the soil. Nothing but the firm determination to win "independence" has spurred the wayfarer to press still further into " the bush," instead of retiring precipitately after this first acquaintance, whose fallacy is soon shown once the rocky barrier has been surmounted. Next, in 1879, came the extension of the railway to this point, and from Gravenhurst the busy lumberman or the busier tourist took steamer to gain the northern parts of the country, and then in 1886 comes the crowning advance of all, the opening of the Pacific Junction Branch right through the heart of the district to the great Lake Nippissing, to Callander, and the connection with the Canadian Pacific.

Later on we will trace the steps of the traveller along this line of railway, but still taking Gravenhurst as the "Gateway City," we will follow first along the water route.

The town occupies a most eligible site, crowning elevated but not too hilly ground, and encircling deep bays with shores sloping down to the water's edge. On the eastern side of the town is *Gull Lake,* a charming little sheet which discharges its waters through the *Hock Rock* trout stream. The place has considerable trade in the manufacture and shipment of lumber and timber. There are three churches ; the stores, hotels and other establishments are creditable in appearance, and supplies of all kinds can be had at extremely moderate prices. The hotels are commodious, well kept and inexpensive. The town is in thriving condition, making fine progress and extending rapidly. The immediate neighbourhood affords considerable attraction to the tourist and sportsman. Brook trout (in limited quantities), salmon trout, bass and pickerel in abundance; deer, partridge, hare and a limited amount of duck shooting—all can be conveniently reached from Gravenhurst as a centre. *Pigeon Lake, Deer Lake,* and *Pine Lake* are reached by the Muskoka road to the north-west.

Loon Lake, Leg Lake, and *Rice Lake* are nearer, and more to the west of the town. *Doe Lake* is about two miles to the east.

The railway station for the town and where the junction for the Callender extension is made, is on the upper level. The lake station, called *Muskoka Wharf*, where connection is made with the Muskoka Navigation Coy's steamers, is reached by a very steep grade winding down a natural gully to the water side. The details of the routes of the steamers is given elsewhere, to which reference should be made.

The Muskosh River Chain.

LAKE MUSKOKA.

This is one of the largest of the lakes comprised under the generic term of "The Lakes of Muskoka," being 22 miles long and 9 miles wide in its extremest points. It is the peculiarity of these lakes that they are so studded with islands that wide open reaches of rough water are scarcely to be met with. This appears to be less the case with Lake Muskoka than with any others ; but its greater size is the only reason, for it teems with islets (as do all its companion lakes), having, in round figures, an island for every day in the year. Its beauties, in detail, are equal to any other lake, but its larger expanse, and the fact that many of its islands are of large size, and have been allowed, in earlier times, to be burned over, take from its picturesqueness. Yet the inhabitants of its islands and shores are enthusiastic in its praises, and vaunt its features as being above all the others. In common with all the lakes of the district, it affords most splendid fishing. The shores are fringed with islands, and salmon-trout are successfully caught by trolling between them; black bass and pickerel abound. One certain advantage it has in accessibility, being the most southerly of all the lakes, so that the visitor coming north arrives earlier and going south leaves later than from any other. But visitors to the Lakes of Muskoka must see, not one, but *all* the lakes; and so we will start from the dock.

To the left is the new village of *West Gravenhurst*, with busy sawmills, and all around the high bluff, granite rocks dipping steeply into the water, so that ample depth exists right alongside their face. Winding between *Percy*, *Henry*, *Mary*, and *Daisy Islands*, we enter another pool, and, after a little, slip through *The Narrows*, where there is bare room for the steamer to pass between the rocks, we enter the broadest part of the lake. On the west point is the lighthouse.

Passing up the centre of the lake, on the east, are *Katago*, *Aultbowrie*, and *Whitt Islands;* while far off to the west are the island settlements of the Denison, Patton, and Moberly families. The largest island is *Browning's Island*. Next, *Eilian-Gowan*, the summer house of Mr. Justice Gowan, comes in view, where art and love of landscape have been called in to assist the attractiveness of Nature, and walks and drives, glades and grottoes, have been formed to make pleasant this holiday country home.

Just opposite this, and winding through the reedy banks which line the shores and forming a sort of delta, are the two mouths of

THE NORTHERN LAKES OF CANADA.

ON THE RIVER.

THE MUSKOKA RIVER.

Entering by an abrupt turn the steamer winds its way up the tortuous channel. Unlike the banks of all other rivers in Muskoka and all other parts, even of itself, the banks of the Muskoka River, between the entrance to the lake and Bracebridge, are soft alluvial deposits of much richness and great depth. The shores are lined to the water's edge with a profusion of rank vegetation and tangled roots of trees or toppled trunks, whose downward branches sweep the surface of the stream. The water is of a dark brown hue and, completely sheltered from the wind, its surface has an oily glassiness, wherein is clearly reflected every bough and little twig, or the white masses of summer clouds that float across the sky above. The river is full of sudden turns; at times the prow appears to be headed direct for the opposing land, when with a sudden sweep the boat is turned almost at right angles, and new vistas with their promontories bathed in sunlight and their cool recesses sunk deep into deeper shadow, come into view.

For six miles turn succeeds to turn; so narrow is the river that we see the surge from the steamer's wheels lay bare the shore, and boats must either be securely fastened to their stakes or else their anxious owners hurry down to keep them from being swept away by the recurrent flood.

At *Alport*, hard by the celebrated "*Munts Farm*," where is the prize-taking herd of Muskoka cattle, we may deliver Her Majesty's mail, and by-and-bye the hills, which we have seen peeping through the vacancies in the forest that fringes the banks, close in, and at the very foot of the "North Falls" is the dock which forms the head of steamboat navigation.

Bracebridge—The chief town of the Muskoka District, and, if not its geographical, yet most certainly its business and county centre. Starting in 1861 with two log huts and their attendant potato patches, and only a fallen pine tree for a bridge over the River, it advanced in 1866 to the proud pre-eminence of three bush stores and a tavern,

106   THE NORTHERN LAKES OF CANADA.

and now may be congratulated upon being a thriving town, with a stirring and fast increasing population, and possessing accommodation for tourists and travellers' which retain it in its position of being the best starting point from which to explore the river district and to

HIGH FALLS.

obtain supplies necessary for the trip. It is true the railway now passes through Bracebridge and runs direct to points beyond, but nevertheless the town has obtained such a lead in its hotel and business advantages, that it will be advisable to continue to avail of them.

THE NORTHERN LAKES OF CANADA. 107

There are five excellent hotels (*see advt.*), Anglican, Methodist, Presbyterian, and Roman Catholic churches. A Mechanics' Institute and Library, and Masonic, and Oddfellows Lodges.

SOUTH FALLS—MUSKOKA RIVER

The town is agreeably situated on the cliffs surrounding the river, and the neighbourhood merits some sojourn from the tourist to visit its interesting surroundings.

At a distance of four miles, either by road or along the bank of the Muskoka river, are the High Falls.

In the summer this group of three falls, which are divided from each other by two islands, are best approached from the right bank. Very little rock is to be seen in the advance to the river, but when it is reached, the visitor, standing on a parapet one hundred feet above the basin, sees on the one side the rushing fall, and then in front from where the curving basin joins again the river bank, stretches out a long straight canal cut by nature's work with steep walls of deepest foliage hemming in its sides. But the chief attraction are the

GREAT SOUTH FALLS.

Above Bracebridge the river is divided into two great branches, each draining a large area of the country. These two unite in the neighbourhood of the town. The Falls of the North Branch are those which are seen from the steamboat landing, but their natural beauty has been sadly interfered with by the necessity of man for bread wherewith to feed, and home wherein to shelter himself and household; thus grist and sawmills abstract the water, and lay bare part of the bed of the stream.

THE UPPER LEAP—SOUTH FALLS.

Having crossed through the town above the North Falls, a walk of about three miles brings one suddenly to the bridge which spans the upper "chute" of the Great SouthFalls. In the level country, when nearing the river, there is nothing to give evidence of the approaching gorge; and from the bridge, as from a perch high up above, we look downward over the mass of tossing, seething foam. It will be noticed that the river, in its descent of a hundred and thirty feet, makes two perpendicular leaps, joined together by upper and by lower pools, in which the waters boil and swirl between their successive rapid descents. To see the Falls to better effect it is well to clamber down over the rough and slippery crags to the foot of the torrent, about 1,000 feet down from the bridge.

The best way, however, to approach this—the most commanding natural feature of Muskoka, and which if it existed in some European country would be considered worth a pilgrimage to visit—is to take canoe down the river from Bracebridge. Shortly after passing Beardmore's Tanneries, the South Branch of the river is entered at a point where a small bridge crosses the entrance. It is a nice row or paddle of three miles to the foot of the Falls. There is one short reach of rapid water, which can be either poled up, or one hundred yards *portage* made. The flecks of foam floating by on the surface of the stream tell of the approaching change of level ; soon the voice of the mighty waters itself is heard ; and in a little while the whole cataract comes full into view. Then, passing through the circling white bells of the eddy foot, we step on shore.

Looking up along the tumultuous snowing mass, the belts of spray at each successive fall hang over the several steps, and sometimes little rainbows enhance the scene. The water is torn into a whitened foam, here and there marked by deep brown streaks where, in deeper spots, it sweeps over some smoother stone. On either side rise the walls of spray-damped solid rock, fringed with young maples and feathered birch, while high above the dark green pines and age-browned bridge stand clear-cut out against the sky.

To facilitate the bringing of the sawlogs down the stream, and prevent their being damaged as they used to be when making the passage of the Falls, the Government has constructed on one bank a "timber-slide," and down this the logs may be seen to run, and tumbling in quick succession, like so many porpoises, into the still waters of the river reach below.

As to the geological action which has formed this cleft, it must, most probably, be classed with those caused by a "fault" or "fissure."

THE GREAT SOUTH FALLS.

The abrading action of either frost or water has been very slight, there being nothing here as in the Gorge of Niagara, capable of being loosened or undermined and the adamantine rocks on either hand repel any great abrasion.

The chasm is like a cleft, wide at the top and contracting towards the water's edge, at one place to about fifteen feet. On the right bank (the left hand side looking up) a vast, almost perpendicular smooth dark, iron-coloured rock is intersected by lighter coloured seams, apparently mixtures of quartz and rosy feldspathic crystals.

The other bank is different, for here crags of what resembles grey sandstone appear in company with others, dazzling the eye by their micaceous glitter.

At the foot of the fall may be noted the bank of pebbles consisting of water-worn stones, from the size of an egg to that of a man's head, of varied colours and all worn smoth—some being actually polished.

Some very remarkable round pockets or cups may also be noticed in the rocks caused by the perpetual rubbing of the imprisoned stones.

The basins of the torrent show plain signs of the laborious friction of the water and the attendant drift, but beyond these and the little bowls before noticed, the centuries have left but little mark upon the barriers of the falls.

From Bracebridge expeditions may be made with facility to Baysville and the Lake of Bays, returning by canoe down the south branch of the Muskoka River, or to the pretty chain of Lakes Vernon, Fairy, and Mary returning from Port Sydney down the North branch, but these will be dealt with further on.

LAKE MUSKOKA AGAIN.

From the mouth of the river, still keeping northward up the lake we pass close to the *Birch* and *Wilson Islands*. Along the high bluff banks may be seen the large encampments of summer visitors, some from other parts of Canada, over which will fly the deep red Union Jack, and others from our neighbours of the United States spreading to the air the more variegated Stars and Stripes.

112 THE NORTHERN LAKES OF CANADA.

Some of these will have groups of eight and ten large tents and reverberating reports from guns will salute the steamer as it passes by

BEAUMARIS.

This, the southermost of the summer resorts of Muskoka, is situated on *Tondern Island*, which, like its progenitor, Anglesea, is separated from the mainland by a narrow channel, the Menai strait. The high square tower of the hotel forms an imposing landmark from all sides. Elevated well above the lake, and with broad continuous verandahs, the hotel is one of the most modern in this district. From the steamer it cannot be seen that in front of the west side is a well cared for tennis ground, or that the very freedom from surrounding obstruction affords unexampled island views extending all over the lake and giving a pleasant outlook from every window, while the shady verandah and free access of the breeze give the coolness so much sought for.

The fishing in the neighbourhood is remarkable, and many long strings of bass grace the hotel kitchen.

Tondern Island has many pretty nooks and bays. The bathing houses are on a nice sand beach near the hotel, and affording perfectly safe bathing for ladies and children. The circuit of the island can be made in a pleasant row of about three miles, passing through the *Menai Straits* and around home again. *Home, Fairholm,* and *The Brothers Islands* are close at hand For rainy days, and these will sometimes come even in Muskoka, the bowling alleys and billiard rooms in a separate house, close by the hotel, will afford pleasant recreation. Like all other Muskoka resorts, fresh air, fine fishing, bathing and boating, are the staple ingredients of the summer holiday, and in opportunity for all these Beaumaris fully abounds. Mr. Prowse, the proprietor of the hotel, has a very large stock of excellent boats both for rowing and sailing (*see advt.*)

Point Kaye is the last point on the east shore of Lake Muskoka before entering the *Indian River,* which forms the connection with Lake Rosseau. The village consists of only a few houses and a post-office.

Immediately opposite Beaumaris, in sight from the hotel, and on the route which the steamer takes when crossing to the western side

H

of the lake, is a cluster of islands known as *The Kettles*, with some-

THE KETTLES.

what of a maze or labyrinth in their many interweaving channels. Among these islands is found the very best bass fishing on the lakes, and splendid trolling for salmon trout. Good guides are advised, as the distances are considerable and acquaintance with the points of the compass necessary for a prompt return to house or camp.

A Specimen Muskoka Letter.

BEAUMARIS, August 10th, 1885.

DEAR TOM,—I wrote you last on my arrival at Toronto, and not caring to spend the balance of my holidays in a city, made up my mind to put in the last week in the far-famed Muskoka Lakes : so went down to Mr. Barlow Cumberland's office on Yonge street, and purchased a ticket for Beaumaris. Off next morning at 8 a.m. per Northern Ry. for Gravenhurst, where I arrived about 1.30. I found a very comfortable steamer waiting to take us up the lakes; had dinner which was served on the boat in first-rate style, and, after about an hour and a half sail up the lake, found myself at Beaumaris. Here I found a first-rate hotel, with capital accommodation. Having secured my room I took a walk round the place to inspect my new quarters. There is a most beautiful view from the front of the house, and a balmy breeze from across the lake was most enjoyable. Some guests were playing tennis on the fine lawn in front, and I purpose putting in part of my time the same way. I then looked up my fishing tackle and got things in order for the next day. Had supper about half past six, then got a boat and took an hour's row to get myself in training. After, returned to the hotel, where I found the folks dancing. There is a large room here which is always ready for that or any like purpose. Next morning, having had lunch put up for me, I started off with a guide for a day's fishing, and commencing just below the hotel, fished along the shores of the island, casting in at all likely spots, and so went on till noon with a result of ten nice bass and three pickerel. We landed at a pretty point, made a fire, got some coffee, cooked sufficient fish for dinner, and I can tell you that is the way to enjoy them, right fresh out of the water into the frying-pan ; I never tasted anything like it before. About half-past three we started again, returning to the hotel for supper with a grand result of thirty-two bass and seven pickerel—not so bad for one day. In the evening played billiards. Next morning, about 9 a.m., the steamer called here on her way to Bala, the outlet of these waters, so I took a trip in her. We first went up to Point Keye P.O., and left the mails, then across to Bala, where we arrived about 10.30. It is a most beautiful spot. There is a fine waterfall, also a large dam where all the logs go over into the river below. Arrived back at the hotel in time for dinner. This is a splendid trip ; the scenery all along the route is simply magnificent. I put in the afternoon playing lawn tennis and bathing ; in the evening there was lots of good music and singing. Next day, after my morning bath, I rowed over to Huckleberry Rock, a place about two miles distant, although only about a mile as the crow flies. It gets its name from the quantity of berries growing upon it, and certainly there is any quantity of them. I climbed to the top of the rock and walked several hundred yards to a place called the Look-out, and here I got one of the finest views I think I ever saw. Nearly the whole of Muskoka Lake and part of Lake Rosseau lay before me, with the islands dotted here and there ; it was a perfect panorama. I returned to the hotel for dinner. In the afternoon I played awn tennis for a while and then went down to the bowling-alley for an hour ; in the evening had a good dance. Next day I and some others took a ramble through the woods as far as Leonard Lake, a very pretty lake about two miles from here. On the way gathered any amount of wild raspberries, also got a lot of pitcher plants. I had never seen any before ; they are very pretty and peculiar. Put in the rest of the day playing billiards and bathing. Next day I spent .ishing with pretty much the same result as before. In the evening there was a concert in the dancing room, which went off very well. Sunday, there was service in the morning and afternoon ; in the evening most of the guests assembled in the music room and had selections of sacred music, sang hymns, etc. On Monday, the proprietor having engaged a steamboat for the day, about fifty guests took a trip up to the head of Lakes Rosseau and Joseph, stopping about an hour at each place. This was truly a delightful sail ; we saw everything at the best advantage, and enjoyed the day thoroughly, getting back to the hotel about 7 p.m., when we found our supper ready for us. I am spending this evening writing you, as I think it is the best opportunity I shall have, as I must get away to-morrow morning. I only wish I could stay here for a month, as I feel 20 per cent. better since I came, and have gained about five pounds in weight. The air is so good and cool I always sleep well at nights, and as for appetite I am afraid to think of it ; I am sure the landlord made very little out of me. I hear several people, who have suffered for years from hay fever, say they have never been so well anywhere as here. In fact they have been quite free from it. Now I must close as I am sure you will be getting tired, and all I can say is that if you want to enjoy yourself and have a real good time, go to Muskoka and spend a week or two.

Yours,

Bon.

BALA.

The east shore of Lake Muskoka is well supplied with islands, but the west shore is very much more so. At present not very extensive hotel advantages exist, but Mr. Thomas Currie has opened a private boarding house for canoeists and campists ; there is no better region than on this west coast of the lake. Most of the islands have been taken up by Torontonians and on many of them houses have been erected. No doubt, when steamboat facilities increase, this region will become as well known as those lying on the more direct routes. *Bala* is a regular fishing centre ; close by are many little lakes among which may be named *Bull, Echo, Clear, Long, Black* and *Hardy's*, but the crowning feature is the *Muskosh River*, which, beginning at this point, carries away the waters of the whole of the vast inland chain of lakes.

MUSKOSH AND MOON RIVERS.

After the stop-log dams erected by the Government for the control of the water of the lake, the stream narrows to a width of about 40 yards, then passing swiftly along for a short distance, gathering, as it were, its energies for the grand leap it now takes over a rocky ledge about twenty-three feet in height. Immediately below the Falls the river widens again, forming powerful eddies, particularly at high water.

Strangers require to exercise extra precaution in the management of their boats or canoes below the portage until the disturbed waters are safely passed, which is only the work of a few minutes.

Descending the river, amid beautiful scenery, are fine bass and pickerel fishing for a distance of about four miles. The channel here divides itself into two streams, the one called the *Muskosh*, the other the *Moon River*, and both discharging their waters into the Georgian Bay through mouths many miles distant from each other.

Numerous falls and rapids interrupt navigation on both streams and no strangers should venture without experienced guides. At the above mentioned dividing point there is really splendid maskinonge fishing; the fish are large and of the finest quality.

Canoes can be taken down the Moon River to Georgian Bay and return made from there by the Crane and Blackstone Lake chains to Lake Joseph or Port Cockburn. (*See the route map.*)

Walker's Point and *Torrance* are hamlets and post offices on the west shore of Lake Muskoka, and in the neighbourhood of the Muskosh River.

THE INDIAN RIVER.

Having sailed up Lake Muskoka, we approach the Northern and upper end of the lake, and, threading our way through the *Seven Sisters* Islands—a cluster not far from Beaumaris—we then pass *Idlewild*, *One Tree*, and *Horseshoe* Islands. On the right hand is seen *Fairmount*. Fairmount is situated one and a quarter miles from Point Kaye, on a pretty bay with a southern aspect, just at the entry of the Indian River. A few families can be accommodated by Mr. Butter, and three cottages can be rented furnished. The little Anglican *Church of the Holy Cross* nestles against the woods in the east corner of the bay; service every Sunday. A sandy beach, sloping gradually down, furnishes perfectly safe bathing for children.

We now enter the converging channel of the *Indian River*. The banks rise high on either side, and the thickly wooded slopes throw dark shadows at the rapid turns, widening out almost into a little lake—some good farms are to be seen upon the shore—and then narrowing up again after a sudden turn, we pass through a channel marked out with fir trees for buoys, and reach the prettiest part of the river. At four miles from Lake Muskoka is

PORT CARLING.

This, of all the villages on the lakes, is the most important—being the most central. Being the converging point for all the steamers running to and fro on the three lakes, access to all parts can most conveniently be obtained from this centre, and frequent communications be kept up with all. The *Stratton House*, most excellently kept by Mr. John Fraser, is very commodious, and has an established reputation. Mr. Vanderbergh's comfortable hostelrie is favourably situated on the garden bank, and has a dock all to itself—(*see advertisement*). Boats and guides to all the fishing and sporting points obtained. There are also very good supply stores, kept by Mr. Wallis and Mr. Hanna—(*see advertisement*)—and three churches. On Sundays, row-boats will be noticed coming from all points, bearing the congregations to divine service Steam launches for visiting the lakes can be hired from Mr. Vanderbergh.

At Port Carling the steamers pass through the locks which connect Lake Muskoka and Lake Rosseau, the latter being four feet the higher level. Transfer is made at the locks from the Lake Muskoka steamer to the side-service steamers running up the different lakes; and tourists are recommended to look closely after their baggage themselves, for, however good any system of checking may be, errors will sometimes occur; and it is little satisfaction either to see your trunk going away on the deck of another steamer, or yourself arriving at your destination to find that your baggage and all your comforts have been left behind. At this transfer point, therefore, have an eye to your baggage yourself.

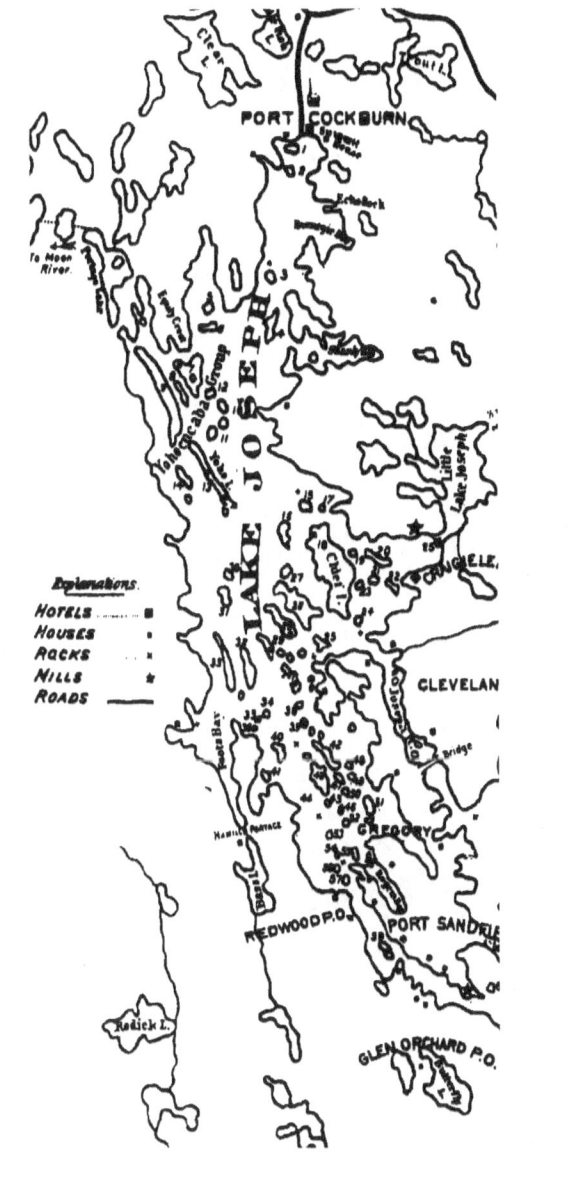

Leaving the village, perched on its picturesque and rugged rocks behind us, we enter a beautiful wooded basin, in which there is most excellent fishing, next passing a point which has been laid out for *Interlaken Park*—a splendid grove for camping and picnicking, and one of the few cases in Muskoka of happy nomenclature. Another turn brings us to the end of the river, and the southern end of the next lake.

LAKE ROSSEAU.

Where the lakes are of such exceedingly irregular form as are all the Lakes of Muskoka, lengths and breadths vary greatly, according to the place from which the measurements are taken. The tourist is usually familiar with lakes which, formed in hollows and basins, have some tolerable regularity of shape ; but these Lakes of Muskoka are unlike any others, being formed, not by any regular depressions of normal strata, but being the upheaval of the old Laurentian system—the oldest geological formation on the continent—which here alone thrusts its head up through the super-imposed masses. Hence the general elevation of the district, and the remarkable changes of shape in the coast lines. Jutting points, deep bays, sudden elongations, and sharp changes of direction, follow quick upon one another, so that the course of the steamer is undergoing constant alteration, instead of proceeding in one general direction following along a somewhat similar shore. It is this constant change which affords such pleasure to the eye on the Lakes of Muskoka ; and though the component parts of the landscape shall be of the same—water, and rock, and tree—yet the ever-changing play of light and form constantly opens out new combinations in colour and beauty of which the sight never wearies nor the interest grows dull.

Lake Rosseau is fourteen miles long in its extremest points. For distances between the several places on this and other lakes, measurements can be made on the maps, which are accurately drawn to a scale of 2½ miles to the inch. After leaving the Indian River, the steamer for *Lake Joseph* diverges to the left, that for *Lake Rosseau* to the right ; and we will first follow up the eastern shore of the lake.

Arthurlie House, about two miles from Port Carling, is ensconced in *Arthurlie Bay*, whose entrance is guarded by a group of pretty islands. There is excellent bass fishing in *Silver Lake*, just behind the house.

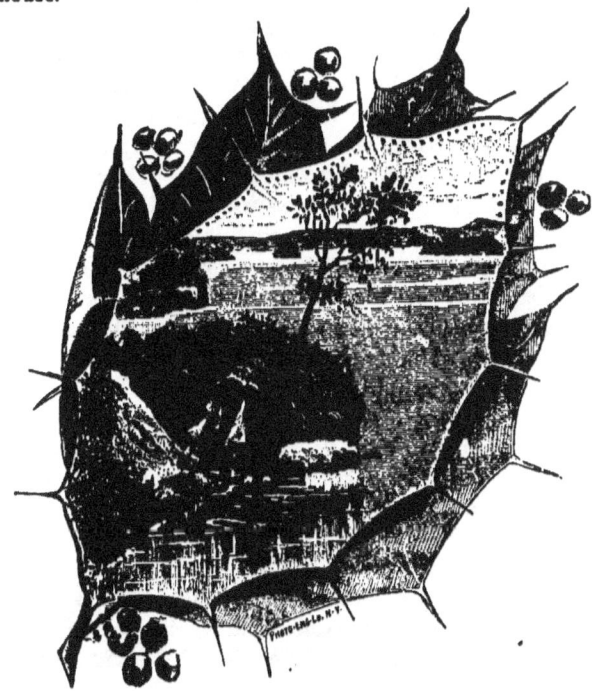

A GLIMPSE ALONG THE COAST.

Brackenrig P. O. lies at the foot of a deep bay. From here a short *portage*, one-quarter of a mile, can be made to *Brandy Lake*, and thence by canoe down *Brandy River* to Lake Muskoka, near Point Kaye and Beaumaris.

Leaving *Baker's, Bohemia, Vacuna,* and *Silver* Islands, and others forming the group at the south point of the island. On a fine bay on the west side of the island is *Cloverport*—a new and attractive summer house.

We now coast up the east shore of *Big* or *Tobin's Island* itself, with high rocks, and, in many places, woods to the water's edge.

Windermere is pleasantly situated on a small bay, four miles from *Port Carling* and ten miles from *Rosseau*. The " *Windemere House*," kept by Mr. Thos. Aitkens, has large accommodation, and increasing business testifies the appreciation of the past endeavours of the proprietor, who, like almost all the other lake-shore hotel-keepers on the lakes, is also the post master and express agent. Hotel-keepers in Muskoka are not only expected to be "Poo-Bahs in offices, but also in information as to all kinds of bait and fish, and where and how to get them. There are plenty of boats kept by the hotel and Mr. J. R. Boyd, and a good bathing place. "The Windermere Mechanics' Institute" has a capital reading room, with a very fair library. A specialty of the neighbourhood is the " Windermere Club," a company which has erected a number of pleasant lake-side cottages which can be rented or purchased, as not a few have been, by families who prefer to "keep house." The resident carpenter, Mr. Clinyboyle, makes repairs and looks after the cottages during the winter months. A very good market held weekly in the summer months, by the farmers in the neighbourhood, insures a cheap and constant supply of fresh provisions.

Ministers of Methodist and Presbyterian churches resides in the village. Pleasant expeditions can be made from Windemere by row boat passing *Florence Island*, the residence of the celebrated actor " Billy Florence," whose Colonel Sellers has become a proverbial type of character, thence to the head of *Portage Bay*,where there is a capital sandy beach.

On going northwards past *Norway Island* to *Dee Mouth* with its saw mill at the outlet of *Dee River*. The mouth of the river is wide and a canoe excursion can be made up it to the Three-Mile Lake, a distance of about two miles with three portages, each of about one hundred yards. It is a pretty woodland walk of two miles to

Dee Bank from where canoeists can take water on the quaint-shaped

THREE-MILE-LAKE.

It may be interesting to note that of the township which contains this lake there is one acre of water to every three of land. There is excellent pickerel fishing in the lake, and its herrings, to be found in shoals near the rocks and banks later on in the fall, are quite famous.

ON THE SHORES OF LAKE ROSSEAU.

There is no regular hotel, but the shores are well settled with thrifty farmers who will welcome visitors. The scenery is much varied and at one point there is a most remarkable echo. *Ella Is-*

land, near the centre, contains the summer residence of Mr. C. McKenzie, of Toronto. It is expected a small steamer will shortly be placed on this lake, but it is a very pretty day's excursion from *Dee Bank*, where is a post office and a capital general store, along the full length of the lake, a distance of eight miles, to *Raymonds Bay*. From here—if the voyagers desire to still further penetrate into the country—canoes can be taken by waggon, making a short cut across the country of about six miles, to join the railway at *Utterson*, and from there to Huntsville, and so take water again on the *Vernon Mary* chain.

Renewing our trip up Lake Muskoka, and having passed the east side of Tobin's Island, a peninsula just out from the west shore, on which is *Juddhaven*, with small dock and post office.

The east shore continues to show sharp promontories and deep bays, the largest, *Skeleton Bay*, about two miles long, and a celebrated fishing point. The entrance is obscured by several islands; at the head is the foot-water of *Skeleton River*, on which are the *Minnehaha Falls*, well worthy a visit, not so much for their magnitude as for their prettiness. Four miles inland is *Skeleton Lake*, another of the larger inland lakes, attractive to venturesome canoeists for its excellent fishing, untrodden islands, many with high cliffs projecting over the water so that boats can be rowed underneath, and its remoteness from the generally travelled routes. The waters are clear like those of Lake Joseph. Considerable portaging has to be done past the rapids and the higher falls to reach its waters, but they can also be conveniently got at in the opposite direction from *Utterson*.

Rosseau Falls is mainly composed of a saw mill and accompanying houses situate at the mouth of the river.

From this on, the banks on the east shore grow in height, and bluff rocks, with deep water at their foot, line the water's edge. At 14 miles from Port Carling we reach the head of the lake.

PORT ROSSEAU.

This village is a place of much importance as it occupies the head of navigation in this direction, and is the starting point for colonization roads leading to Parry Sound and Nippissing and the many settlements situated along their lengths. Post and telegraph offices keep up communication with the southern world, and there are some good stores, particularly for hardware and fishing tackle.

Pratt's Hotel, which stood on a well elevated situation, but was destroyed by fire one autumn, used to monopolize a large portion of

ON THE SHADOW RIVER.

the tourist business, and so great was the satisfaction of visitors with the amusements and the beauty of the environs of this part of the ake, that attention was almost wholly directed to it, and it was not until the withdrawal of the hotel accommodation having obliged visitors to seek other points of sojourn, that the world woke up to the knowledge that there were many other beautiful spots on the shores of the lakes, and that as each had its own peculiar attractions and advantages, it was best to *see them all.*

The waters about Rosseau are well stocked with fish, and abundant and pleasant boating can be enjoyed.

The *Monteith House* is well situated near the steamboat wharf, and among the amusements of the village is a roller skating rink.

The Shadow River, one of the most wonderful natural curiosities of the Muskoka district, empties its waters into the bay on the shores of which Port Rosseau stands. Its course can be explored inland by boats for about five miles, the stream varying throughout from twenty to sixty feet in width. Entering the mouth of the river, about the time of the fast declining rays of the afternoon sun, and following the erratic curves, all sight of the lake is soon lost. In front and behind, the river winds like a silver streak, hemmed in on either hand by forest trees, and losing itself in the distant curves. Tall elms and ranks of tapering pines line the banks, and below them the sedgy shores, heavy with foliated ferns and wreaths of moss, overhang the edge. The surface is as motionless as glass and everything is duplicated in marvellous detail, each leaf and branch having its reflected counterpart even more distinct than it appears itself.

" The fair trees look over, side by side,
And see themselves below."

In the deep silence which pervades the place and affects the onlooker as he gazes at the magic scene, a wonderful illusion creeps over his absorbed senses. Gradually the river's surface fades away, double lines of forest trees array the shores, their stems divided in the centre, the one part pointing upward to the sky, the other reaching downward until in fairy vision the vacancy of spaceless depth is bounded far away beneath by mountains of snowy clouds in setting of azure blue. The boat appears suspended in mid-air, half-way between two zenith heavens, and at every stroke of the dripping oar would seem as though upon the verge of being plunged into a bottomless abyss.

Peering silently over the side, eternity lies spread before the gaze, at all sense of earthliness is lost, while the eye searches the passing glimpses of what looks to be another world......A merry laugh or the swoop of the king-fisher, as he seeks his finny prey, will recall the dreamer to his senses, but leave a profound impression of a strange and eyrie sensation that elfs and fairies may have been about.

> "For there are haunts in this fair land,
> Ah ! who may dream or tell
> Of all the shaded loveliness
> That hides by grot and dell."

On a small tributary of the Shadow River, the *Bridal Veil Falls* by delicate feathery cascade, makes silver music in its forest grove, and a visit perchance may give some hesitating anxious swain an opportunity of freeing from his halting tongue the words which cleave so closely to his heart.

Half a mile from the village and on a projecting point, giving long vistas up and down the lake, is the new hotel,

MAPLEHURST.

The high gabled roof and broad eaves projecting like those of some Swiss chalet, are prominent objects long before the steamer reaches the little dock.

Harry Ditchburn's fleet of boats and canoes clustered around the landing place invite to frequent water trips, and the cool shades of the surrounding grove of evergreen and silver birch, or lounges on the spacious verandah, 200 feet in length, may tempt to more lazy methods of passing over the hours of the happy summer days. A ferry to the dock in the village keeps up constant communication, and mails and telegraphs are delivered at the Hotel (*see adv.*).

It is a very pretty walk of 1½ miles through the forest, from Rosseau to *Ashdown*, the junction of the main roads ; or a drive of 10 miles passing a succession of pretty little lakes, lands the traveller at Port Cockburn, at the head of Lake Joseph. Carriages can be engaged in the village. A stage runs regularly 23 miles to Parry Sound.

At many of the rocky points, from one to six miles down the main Lake Rosseau, there is good fiishing for Bass, Pickerel and Salmon Trout.

THE BRIDAL VEIL FALLS.

Morgan's Bay, a large estuary opening from the main lake a little south from *Maplehurst*, is studded with many islands and several deep-recessed bays. In the north bay a portage of ¼ mile enters *Sucker Lake*, and in the south bay a 100 yards portage leads to *Bass*

Lake. Both of these are well stocked. There are also a whole series of small lakes to the north beginning with *Turtle Lake*, the head waters of the Shadow River, reached best by a drive of six miles from Rosseau. Connected with this by short portages are several other lakes where sport is certain. Good speckled trout fishing can be enjoyed in *White Oak Creek* and its tributaries, and in several of the lakes connected with it, easily reached by road five miles from Rosseau. *Blackstone Lake* is reached by daily stage to Pender's Corners, and then a drive of four miles down the side road. It is better not to attempt these more distant excursions without experienced guides. There are many other small lakes containing good fish, but not so accessible as those named. These can be reached by the aid of Indians and birch bark canoes. Indians can be hired through Ditchburn Bros. at about $2 per day including use of canoe. The active canoeist, who is making the tour of the lakes, can, instead of returning down the main Lake Rosseau, make a very interesting short cut to *Lake Joseph*. At the west side of *Morgan's Bay* there is a much frequented portage of ½ mile to *Little Lake Joseph*. This makes a varied and novel expedition for parties with light canoes and camping equipment, and saves the necessity of doubling any portion of their trip.

Returning to the foot of the lake we will join the steamer for *Lake Joseph*, which, on leaving the Indian River, turns to the left, heading for *Port Sandfield*, distant on the direct route six miles from Port Carling, although this is generally prolonged by many calls at the intermediate islands.

Venetia.

This southern portion of *Lake Rosseau* is fairly gemmed with islets, and as they were early selected for their beauty and admirable situation, more island population has been accumulated in this part than in any other. On almost every island can be seen some pretty home, each varied by the tastes or fancies of the owner. Home-made architecture and amateur carpentering have put some together out of the materials to be found on the spot; others have called in more specially instructed aid, but none are at all pretentious. Comfort rather than display, simplicity and make-the-best-of-it seem to be the ruling influences among the "Muskokans." They are clannish in their upholding of the special beauties of the vicinity in which they are settled, but national in united assertion that there is *no* place like Muskoka. Hospitable they certainly are, and to overflowing, for when the steamer touches at their islands, and one sees the number of people and babies that run down to the dock, and the number of heads that pop out of the windows of the house itself, one wonders where they all put up, and whether some, like the Indians, wrap themselves in blankets and sleep beneath the spreading trees. But another turn of the wheel and the white ridge of a tent or the clustering poles of a wigwam, tell where the boys—and what boys the Muskoka boys are—have overflowed to make room for the welcome guests.

This lower part of Lake Rosseau may well be called "*Venetia*," for a boat is as necessary to a man as a pair of legs, and not in Venice itself are boats more used or needed. Whether it be to make a call on a neighbour, to bring the bread from the baker, or fuel for the fire, or fish for the pot, a boat is always put in requisition, so that the Muskokans might almost be considered an amphibious race. They *all* row, from the smallest baby upwards, and *La Belle Canadienne*, who in winter has been seen in picturesque toboggan suit, with bright rosed cheeks, flushed by the keen vigour of her native air, will here be met again with those same cheeks bronzed to a ruddy brown and handling the oars of her boat with all the grace and deftness of an adept. No wonder Canada's oarsmen lead the world! *Vive la Canadienne!*

On the south point of Tobin's Island is the new hotel, *Oaklands*, which, being just opposite to all the many islands of *Venetia*, is sure to afford a pleasurable summer outing.

Ferndale is an excellent hotel, kept by Mr. Penson, and on a pretty bay, into which the steamer turns. The summer-houses on

VENETIA.

the high cliffs have before them one of the most beautiful views of the lakes, and the groves of oak and maple, the virgin forest of hardwood trees in the rear, give opportunity for pleasant walks. The steamer then threads her way through the island homes of "Venetia." To the right is *St. Leonard's Isle* and the "Parson's Group," where the relatives of two reverend gentlemen of Toronto have established themselves, and clerical friends are right royally welcomed. On the left are in succession *Edith, Fairview, Summerside, Gouldings*, then *Oak and Flora*, the pretty home of Dr. Hall, one of the earliest and most enthusiastic of the Muskokans. Still farther away, on the right, *Cedar Island*, the property of Mr. C. S. Warren ; then *Mazengah*, the home of the Dwights and Blatchfords, and *Fairylands*, the Lilly homestead. Lastly we turn sharply round *Olive Island*, where so deep is the water and sheer the rock that the steamer runs alongside without need of any dock. Here the Baldwins early found a happy resting place, and by practice, learned how to fell trees so that they should not fall, as did an early one they cut, squash down upon their newly erected house to its complete destruction. A mute protest, perchance, from the forest king against the innovations made into his realm.

Passing the lofty headland of *Eagle's Nest*, the lake narrows up and we are soon in view of *Port Sandfield*.

The steamer runs to and fro, calling at the different islands and also crosses to the northerly side of the lake. At about two miles is *Cleveland's ;* a summer boarding house is kept here, by Mr. Minnett, with excellent accommodation. Further down the shore, to the east, Mrs. Lawson takes boarders. Mr. Wood's boarding house at *Fair-View-Farm* is about a mile to the west, with a nice sand beach and dock, at which the steamers land. All these localities are in the vicinity of good fishing, and being a little out of the regular route, are perhaps more quiet and retired, and favourable arrangements can be made for short visits or lengthened stay.

Gregory is just at the entrance of the Joseph River, has a post-office, and some of the residents in the neighbourhood will accommodate summer visitors.

PORT SANDFIELD.

At one time a narrow spit, or bar, of sand, here separated Lake Rosseau from Lake Joseph, but in the interests of continuous steamboat navigation a canal was dug through it by the Ontario Government, and the new village which sprung up was named after the

EAGLE'S NEST, LAKE ROSSEAU.

then Premier—the Hon. Sandfield Macdonald—as the point where the junction was made between Lakes Muskoka and Rosseau had been named after the then Commissioner of Crown Lands, the Hon. John Carling. Originally Lake Joseph was 1½ feet the higher, but now both lakes are of the same level. A lofty bridge, spanning the canal, keeps up the communication by road with Port Carling.

PORT SANDFIELD.

On the top, or saddle, of the promontory, and with views extending east and west over both the lakes, is *Prospect House*, kept by the characteristic Enoch Cox. So great is the desire to stay at this favoured spot that although each year its capacities have been enlarged, until now there are rooms for 120 visitors, yet the cry is "still they come." Pleasant verandahs and shady groves covering the tops of rocky points, fifty and sixty feet above the level of the water, form pleasant lounging places. Bathing can be enjoyed from the rocks in an adjacent bay, or from the bathing-houses, which are situated on a pleasant sandy beach. Row-boats can be hired from Mr. Cox by the day or week at low rates, and the steam yacht, built, owned, and captained by Mr. John Rogers—the "hydrographer of the lakes"— leaves the hotel every morning for the points of interest in the neighbourhood, which enables visitors to take delightful excursions out of the regular track of the mail steamers. Special charters can be made on very reasonable terms. The belfry of the Anglican church will be seen near the hotel; service is held regularly every Sunday.

There are several cottages, which may be rented, and summer boarding-houses, in the vicinity—among them *Rockhurst*, just on the opposite side of the bay, kept by Mr. G. C. Hazelwood, well situated and supplied with boats. There is a pretty walk through the woods, 1½ miles, to Port Carling.

LAKE JOSEPH.

This, the third of the series of the Lakes of Muskoka, was for a long time a *mare incognitum* except to the venturesome spirits, who, recking not the labour, rowed themselves up its length of fourteen miles, when the steamer used to be stopped by the natural barrier at Port Sandfield.

It will be noted that the waters of all the other lakes and rivers of Muskoka are, although translucent and clear, yet of a dark or tawny hue, while, strangely enough, those of Lake Joseph are a clear white. Its islands, too, rise perhaps more abruptly, and to higher elevations, and more rugged cliffs line its shores, than do those of the other lakes. Backed by these peculiarities, the inhabitants of the Canton of Lake Joseph claim for it a beauty surpassing that of all the others. This at least may be granted, that it has characteristics, such as those mentioned, unique and peculiar to itself; but so have all the lakes, and this is one of the inexhaustible charms of the Lakes of Muskoka district.

Very nice jaunts, with excellent fishing, can be enjoyed from Port Sandfield. A row up Lake Joseph of three miles to *Hemlock Point* and the lines having been cast in around the group of fish-named islands off the point, or on a row down *Avon* and *Cumberland Bays* will surely be rewarded by a good catch.

Bass Lake is best reached by Rogers' steam yacht to *Foot's Bay*, a distance of about seven miles; from here a *portage* of a quarter of

LAKE JOSEPH.

a mile brings to the lake. Mr. T. Hamill, whose house is near by, keeps boats upon the lake, and is recommended for supplying guides. The lake is carefully preserved, and well stocked with fish.

A very pretty round trip can be made by towing the row-boats behind the yacht up Lake Joseph, and past *Fisher, Foster*, and *Canifi Islands*, to the upper end of the *Joseph River*, near by the prettily situated *Craigie-Lea*. From here the boats can be rowed down the river through channels too narrow and shallow for even the little steamer. A beautiful succession of changes of direction and surprises follows, for a distance of three miles, to the exit into Lake Rosseau, near *Gregory's*. Two miles further, and the party is home again at Prospect House. The whole distance round can be rowed by a vigorous oarsman in about five hours, or the journey can—as is most pleasant—be broken for the night at

CRAIGIE-LEA.

Before the cutting of the Port Sandfield Canal, this Joseph River was the only means of water communication between the lakes, and, being very tortuous, was available only for small boats. Nestled in behind the *Ponemah Group* of islands, and on a pretty projecting point of land, Mr. John Walls has placed his new hotel—*(see advertisement)*. The situation is most unique for quiet and retirement; the surrounding shores are all as Nature first, in simple beauty, decorated them with her unerring hand; and sheltered passages wind between the islands in constantly changing forms.

AROUND CLIFF ISLAND.

Just in front is the particularly beautiful *Cliff Island*. Green slopes, looking in the distance as though of softest, smoothest turf, rise from the water's edge to the rounded top, about two hundred feet in height. Studded at intervals over these are regularly shaped groups of evergreens—the rich-toned Norway and the dwarf Northern pine. No landscape gardener ever posed his groups with more effective result; nor could he, with all his art, attain to such unstudied loveliness as here exists. Just to the right of the hotel is the entrance to *Little Lake Joseph*, sometimes fondly termed *Little Joe*. No settlers have yet occupied its untrodden shores, and there is splendid fishing in its waters. At the head of the lake—seven miles from Craigie-Lea—is the landing for the half-mile *portage* to Morgan's Bay, and thence three miles by water to Maplehurst and Rosseau.

Resuming the direct route up the centre of Lake Joseph, from Port Sandfield the steamer calls first at *Redwood*, the admirably situated summer home of the Ardaghs. Leaving Foot's Bay on the left, we thread our way through the Ponemah Group, comprising the largest islands in the lake. On the shores of "Chief Island" is the homestead of Herbert Mason, Esq. ; and on "Governors Island," a beautiful little islet commanding a lovely view over the length of the open lake, is the summer residence of the Hon. John Beverley Robinson, the Lieutenant-Governor of Ontario. The shores stretch wider apart, and then comes another series called the *Yo-ho-cu-ca-ba Group*. A thoroughly Indian intonation would appear to attach to this name, with its constantly repeated vowel sounds, and one wonders as to what may be its native meaning. It is a revelation to be told that it was framed from the first syllables of the names of the first occupants of the largest island. Thus :—

Yo	Professor Young.
Ho	W. H. Howland.
Cu	Montgomery Cumming.
Ca . . .	Professor Campbell.
Ba . . .	James Bain.

This group are as largely populated as any parts of the lakes ; and the Sunday services, held in a natural amphitheatre on "Yoho," as the principal island is lovingly called, have acquired a provincial celebrity from the standing of the preachers who have officiated at them, under the canopy of the forest trees.

Mr. McMurrich's completely-developed island, where the Marquis of Lansdowne, Governor-General of Canada, sojourned in 1885, is passed on the left; then *McLellan's* and *Wahneshing*, and the lofty *Equity Crest*. After the beautifully-shaped *Round Island*, we enter the last bay, and come into view of the end of the trip in this direction.

PORT COCKBURN.

This is the head of navigation of Lake Joseph. Upon a high

cliff, and surrounded by a beautiful grove of second growth oak and maples, so that only the gables can be seen, is the Summit House, well kept by Hamilton Fraser, now the largest house in the district. Between the trees and on the sides of the rocks where convenient nooks give opportunity, are swinging hammocks and rustic seats, and from the ample height and pleasant shade, a lovely view overlooking the island-studded lake can be most fully grasped and thoroughly enjoyed.

The steamer lands at the foot of the stairways leading up to the hotel. Near by is seen the *Island Park*, where a grove has been set out with winding paths and a bridge built to connect the island with the main land. On the other side of the hotel is a splendid bathing house and sheer rocks from which the bolder ones can spring into fifty feet of water.

The ubiquitous Ditchburn Bros. here again appear with a full line of excellent row boats, from small ones for those with whom "two is company and three is none" to the large family ark wherein the good-natured Father, having stowed his substantial partner together with all their merry flock of chattering youngsters, can swelter at the unaccustomed oar in full enjoyment of his summer holiday of *rest*.

About fifteen minutes' row from the hotel are the celebrated "Echo Rocks" where in the mysterious moonlight hours weird repetitions may be evoked.

"Hark! how the gentle echo from her cell,
Talks through the cliffs and murmuring o'er the stream
Repeats the accents "we-shall-part-no-more."
—*Akenside.*

It is a pretty trip also to "Hawk's nest," and to the little bay and portage to *Byers Lake*.

Post and telegraph offices in the hotel and a large room for concerts and dancing ensure plenty of amusement for the summer evenings.

Port Cockburn is the centre of a great many fishing resorts to which access can from it most conveniently be obtained. Guides and canoes can be arranged for with Ditchburn and bait provided.

Lake Joseph abounds with black bass, pickerel and large salmon trout obtained by deep trolling.

Within a radius of six miles from the Summit House, there are some forty little lakes, some reached by driving and many by walks through the "bush," and in the tributary streams brook trout are often canght weighing 1½ pounds.

The *Seguin River Chain* begins a few miles back from here and comprises a complete chain of lakes and river to Parry Sound on the Georgian Bay. *White Fish*, *Clear*, *Turtle*, *Star* and *Isabella* are the principal ones, and in all black bass and trout abound. *Blackstone* and *Crane* lakes, which are five miles off (see the route map to Moon River), may best be described by taking the statement of Battelle in the Toledo "*Po* ":

"The shores of Crane and ... stone Lakes are capital specimens of the primitive wilderness, an ... may they so continue. The few who have visited their teeming waters have mostly been genuine fishermen who are happiest when far away from conventionalities and habitations. But one clearing broke the majestic sweep of the grand old forests, within the sheltered bays the loons laughed undisturbed, and the wild birds splashed in the marshy edges or upon the sandy shores with none to molest or make them afraid.

"We were out for maskinonge, and took no account of either black bass or pickerel. It seems strange to talk of shaking off black bass and making disrespectful remarks about these gamy gentry when they insisted in taking the hook, but they were so plenty as to be really troublesome.

"When an angler goes forth to catch the maskinonge it is necessary to be careful lest the maskinonge should catch him. The native method of taking the maskinonge in the primeval waters of Canada is by a small clothes line, hauled in by main strength when the fish bites, but we proposed to troll, as should an angler, with the rod. Ours were split bamboo rods 9½ feet long, quadruplex reel, and braided linen line, two feet of medium sized copper wire, a No. 4 spoon with double hooks, and finally a good gaff.

"Our guide, as we started over to *Crane Lake* the first morning, indulged in sundry smiles and remarked that we should break our rods, so that, although placid in outward mien, I felt inwardly a little nervous, but I didn't mean to back down until compelled.

"Swinging around a little point, with some twenty yards of line astern, before fishing a great while I felt a sudden movement at the spoon that was more like a crunch than a bite. It took only a second to give the rod a turn that fixed the hooks and another second to discover that I had hung something. Scarcely had I tightened the line when the fish started. I do not know that I wanted to stop him, but I felt the line slip rapidly from the reel as though attached to a submarine torpedo. The first run was a long one, but the line was longer, and the fish stopped before the reel was bare. This was my opportunity and I had the boatman swing his craft across the course, and reeling in the slack line, I turned his head towards the deeper water. Forty-five minutes of as pretty a fight as one cou.d wish to see left my new acquaintance alongside the boat, and before he recovered his surprise the gaff was in his gills and the boatman lifted him on board.

"He weighed fourteen pounds on the steelyards and was m; heaviest fish. There were other encounters of a similar character, but none quite so protracted; but I wouldn't be afraid of the largest veteran in the lake, and all fishermen, who aim for sport, will assuredly troll with the rod. Our time was limited, far too short, and in a word, a day and a half on Crane Lake gave us, without counting bass, ten maskinonge whose weight aggregated 110 pounds, (on the scales) an average weight of 11 pounds per fish."

THE MOON RIVER.

The lower reaches of these famed waters, where they enter the Georgian Bay, can conveniently be attained by the route of these lakes as shown on the detailed map, or, having descended the river by canoe from Lake Muskoka at *Bala* (the easier mode), return can be made by them to Lake Joseph, at Port Cockburn.

The fishing scores in the Moon River, particularly maskinonge, are of the heaviest, and some giants have been hooked.

This expedition should not be attempted without good guides and ample camping equipment and supplies.

The New Railway.

Gravenhurst to Lake Nipissing.

Having followed the shores of the group of the BIG TRIO and traced their waters to the outfall by the *Muskosh* and *Moon Rivers*, we will strike further inland to the newer districts which are now opened out for convenient access by the new extension of the railway through their midst. Starting afresh from *Gravenhurst* (page 101), the railway strikes inland along the shores of *Gull Lake*, and after crossing the south branch of the Muskoka River, reaches *Bracebridge* (10¼ miles). (The mileages here and afterwards mentioned are mileages from Gravenhurst.)

Here the iron bridge spans the stream above the very midst of the Falls—a strange situation ; but the defiles through which railways in this district may be constructed are exacting, and their behests must be obeyed, however, unusual the forced selections. Still keeping in the valley alongside the river at about two miles beyond Bracebridge, a very pretty view is obtained, on the right of *Elliott's Falls.*

Utterson (24 miles)—Connection can be made from here by good waggon road to *Skeleton Lake* or else to *Three Mile Lake*, and by either route convenient voyage made by their waters to those of Lake Rosseau, not far from *Windermere.*

Two and a half miles to the east by road is *Port Sydney*, at the southern end of *Mary Lake*, to which we will make a visit farther on.

After a passing glimpse at *Little Round Lake*, the train arrives at *Huntsville* (35 miles). This is an important tourist point, as here connection is made with a new chain of lakes, whose waters may be followed, either west to their source, or east and south until they are drained by the Muskoka River. The village is progressing, and will, no doubt, soon have its full share of the increase business which the railway now brings to its doors. Jacob's Hotel, Gilchrist's and Birtch's Hotels, are mentioned here.

The Muskoka River Chain.

WESTWARD TO THE HEADWATERS.

Alongside the railway station will be found the steamboat dock, at which can be taken, for the trip up the lakes, the steamer *Northern*, Captain Denton. Should our *voyageurs*, however, have so prepared themselves, and intend to start off on one of the many canoeing trips which radiate from here, their traps and camping equipment will be quickly packed away, and soon

"'Their *bark* is on the sea."

After about three miles of open river navigation, *Lake Vernon* is entered. On the right bank will be seen where the waters of the Upper North Branch enter the lake. *Hood's Island* is passed on the left, and, the lake widening out again, the village of *Ravenscliff* is called at. Here enters the stream which brings down the waters of *Loon* and *Long Lakes*. At 9 miles the lake ceases; and we arrive at the head of steamboat navigation in this direction.

HOODSTOWN.

The town is situated at the outlet of the upper waters, and a splendid water-power has been formed, which, no doubt, some day will turn some busy wheels, if its owner will only allow it to be used. There is a waterfall of about 40 feet in height over the mill-dam. The *Albion Hotel*, kept by J. G. Henderson, and the *McCallum House* are spoken of as good hostelries. There are good roads in the neighbourhood, and a large adjacent population. Near by, and rising abruptly above the plain, is *Mount Ararat*. The bluff is 500 feet above the highest parts of the land; its top is flat, and if the Ark did not stop here it may at least have touched.

From the summit the wood-clad landscape may be seen, waving for miles around, in billows of massy green fading into distant blue, and upon its front, set like so many precious gems, are to be counted the surfaces of fifteen little lakes, reflecting in their rippling waters the bright rays of the summer sun.

Having examined the neighbourhood, the trip to the head waters of the chain is recommenced. It is a short portage through the town from *Lake Vernon* to the foot water of *Fox Lake*, so called from the shape of its shores taking a figure very much the outline of a fox. It is about three miles to the narrows, between the body and the tail. At the end of the lake the *Buck River* is entered. The river runs smooth and deep, between 30 and 40 feet wide. The banks are steep and high, showing signs of excellent soil, and there are many picturesque turns in the route of five miles. There is one short rapid which going up must be passed by a portage of 100 yards, but coming down can be run with safety. Next is entered *Buck Lake*, six miles long and of narrow but varying width. On its shores is *Ilfracombe* with saw and grist mills, and the centre of an English colony of high county standing and much cultivation.

The pretty Anglican church is well maintained, and as far as can be, brings back fond memories of services in the ivy-clad fanes of the fatherland. At the head of the lake a small stream is entered, and after one mile access is made to *Round Lake*, itself 2½ miles long. Another stream nearer the foot of Buck Lake leads by a route of about six miles, in which there is one rapid, which must be portaged both ways, to *Axe Lake*, itself 2½ miles long. These two lakes, Axe and Round, are the head waters in this direction of this chain of lakes. From Huntsville to here (26 miles) row boats can be used; and there is no better or safer line of route for a pleasant camping and boating trip, combining both lake and river accessible to all.

Throughout these upper waters and in the tributary streams there is excellent trout fishing. Our voyageur will either return from here, or, if his equipment permit its transport, may make a portage of three miles over the water-shed which here forms the dividing line, and embark his craft upon the waters of *Doe Lake*, a tributary to the headwaters of the *Maganetewan River*. Proceeding down this for nine miles he will join the railway again at *Katrine* (55 miles).

And in penetrating to the interior all this may here be found, but without the necessity of going too far away from the centres of habitation.

"'There is a pleasure in the pathless woods,
There is a rapture on the lonely shore,
There is society where none intrudes."

Down Stream to Bracebridge.

By the North Branch.

From *Huntsville* the voyageur returning down the river to join the railway again at Bracebridge, or farther on at Gravenhurst—has two routes open to his choice the one by the *North*, the other by the *South* branch of the Muskoka River.

In taking the first, the steamer can be availed of, passing through the pretty *Fairy Lake*, (five miles) and then the river again is entered.

For the furtherance of navigation, a lock has been constructed by the Ontario Government, near Fetterley's and by this means, after three miles more of river navigation, winding and re-winding throughout, the next lake of the chain is reached.

Mary Lake is one of the gems of Muskoka; many neat residences with clearings of some extent adorn its shores. Its surface is studded with many islands, where berries of various kinds are plentiful in the season, and afford delightful places for pic-nics and camps. At the foot of the lake, upon a gentle elevation overlooking its length, is *Port Sidney*. The village contains the Sydney Hotel, where there is excellent accommodation provided by Mr. Jeff Avery. A good supply of boats is kept and pleasant trips can be made upon the romantic little lakes. From Port Sidney, return to the railway can be made by two and a half miles drive to the station at *Utterson*.

For those who do not venture on small boating or canoeing, the steamboat route between Hoodstown and Port Sydney, upon the "Little Trio," *Vernon*, *Fairy* and *Mary*, will make a very pretty excursion and give additional zest to the enjoyment of the larger and more well-known lakes.

Those, however, who do "canoe," can take the Muskoka River from Port Sydney, and enjoy the unique sensation of "running a rapid." In the route of fifteen miles to Bracebridge, there are some of

the
has
by

ugh
is

1 by
after
ugh-

nces
tud-
tiful
At
gth,
here
good
ro-
be

the
the
etty
and

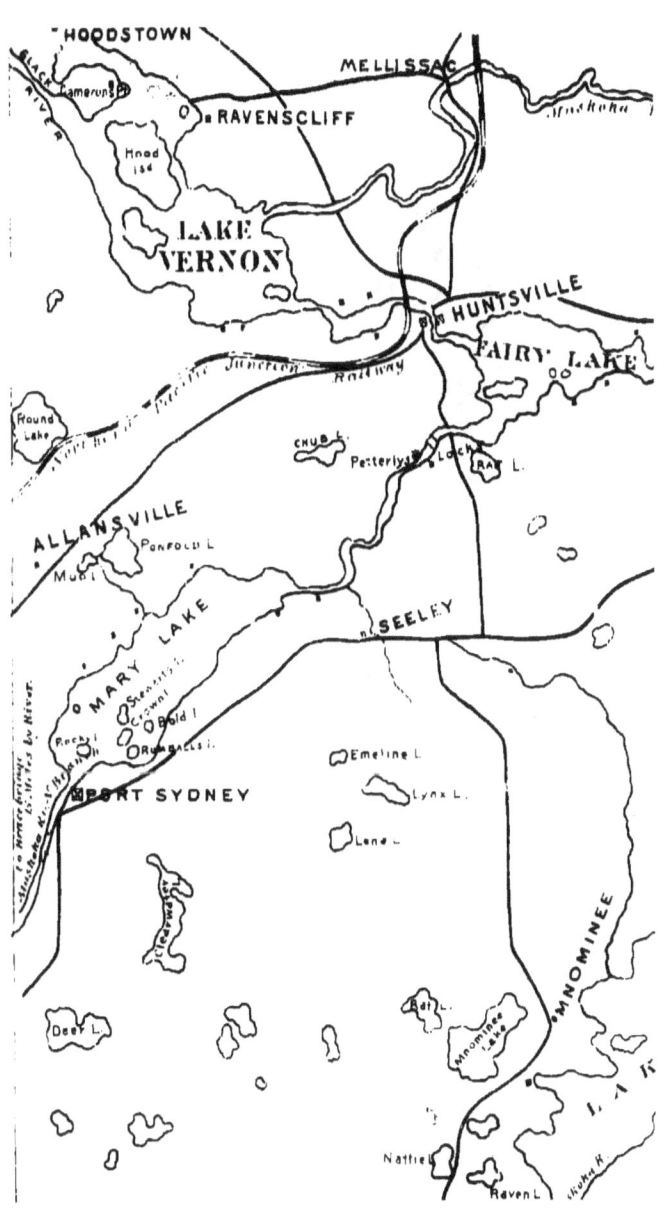

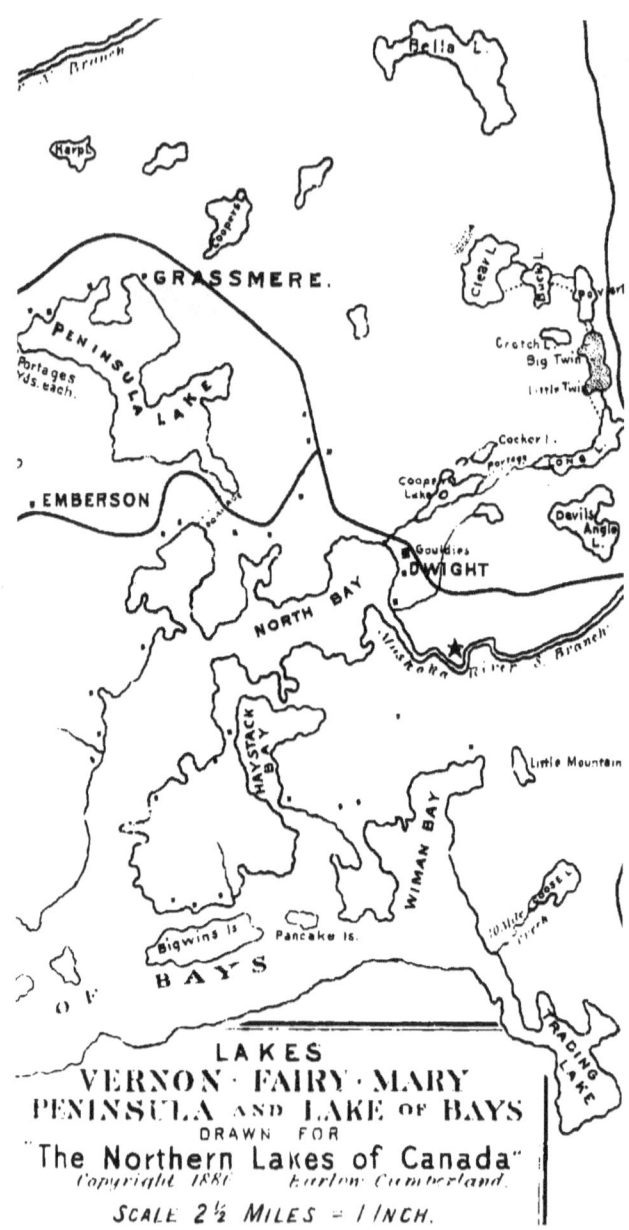

the rapids which it is not safe to run, but which must be portaged. The entrances to all are well marked so that a watchful eye will keep the canoe from danger. It will be best to leave in the morning and then the run through can be made in the day

By the South Branch.

The other choice of route in returning from Huntsville is confined to canoeists.

Passing easterly through the length of Fairy Lake, a narrow is entered, in which are two portages, each of one hundred feet length on the right or south bank, and thus access is obtained to *Peninsula*

RUNNING A RAPID—MUSKOKA RIVER.

Lake. On the north shore is *Grassmere* post-office, and : ne southeast end (seven miles), a portage of 1½ miles brings ⁺ the *Lake of Bays*. The convenience of a waggon will easily be o'tained from some neighbouring settler. Thence to Baysville, at t foot of the lake, is twelve miles, and from there, twenty-five miles by river to the south branch of the Muskoka to Bracebridge. Some people may prefer to go up stream, so we will start with them from Bracebridge. It may be well for the canoeist who is making his first acquaintance with these river waters, to begin by going up stream, as he will thus become acquainted with the indications of rapids, and by no chance run himself into danger. The *South Branch* of the Muskoka is the starting point for some of the best fishing districts of Muskoka, among others are *Walter's Creek*, *Hollow Lake*, *Wood Lake*, *Sharp's Creek*,—all celebrated for their brook trout.

A stage runs regularly from Bracebridge to *Baysville* (16 miles), leaving on arrival of the mail trains and arriving in the evening.

Leaving Bracebridge by water, the tourist can either descend the Muskoka River by canoe to the " River Forks," thence up the South Branch to the foot of the " Great South Falls," where the first port-

MAKING A PORTAGE—MUSKOKA RIVER.

age must be made, or, bringing the canoes and camping equipment by waggon, can at this same point commence the ascent of the river.

The stream is rapid, and several portages must be made during the first day. At some the baggage is carried round by land and the canoes poled up the rapid; at others, the Indians shoulder the canoes, thus presenting the appearance of huge snails. At " Rocky Portage" good ground is found for the first " camp." On the second day, " Island Portage " is reached at noon, and " Gravelly Rapids " for the night. At both of these points there is good trout fishing.

On the third day "Cedar Rapids" are passed, and at the "Upper Falls" near Baysville, the best camping ground is found. The river here runs fast, tumbling down in rocky rapids, and the best speckled trout fishing afforded.

Baysville, on the river and 1½ miles from the entrance to the lake, is a capital resort for the tourist and the sportsman. Those who are on the round trip will find it about a day's canoeing from the "Upper Falls," to the camping ground at the portage to Peninsula Lake; from thence they can proceed, as previously described. There are good local supply stores in the town, and arrangements for steamboat trips on the lakes can be made with Capt. Huckins. Jelly's Hotel; the Norfolk House, kept by Mr. Howard, and Keeler's Hotel are mentioned here.

LAKE OF BAYS.

This is the largest of the lakes which are tributary to the Muskoka River, being about 20 miles in length. In width it is eccentric and fully deserves its name. There are not many islands in it, but it is superlative in jutting points, clad with the dark green outlines of the finest pine timber. Canoeists who are exploring its shores, had better, after taking the south east trip towards *Dorset*, return north by *Haystack Bay*, and make the short portage to North East Bay. As not having been so accessible, the shores of its deep clear waters remain more in the state of nature than any other. Neither the settler's axe nor the fires of careless camping parties have denuded the banks of their leafy coverings.

CAMP FIRES.

How earnestly it is to be wished, that all who light "camp-fires" would be watchful to see that all sparks are perfectly extinguished. Oftentimes it will appear to the eye that no fire remains, but underneath, in the dry mossy ground, a "smudge" still exists to burst long after into flame, and spreading slowly through the roots and undergrowth to do infinite damage.

Never light a fire except upon bare rock or bare ground—if on the latter, remove all neighbouring moss, so that the fire cannot by any means spread.

Always before leaving put the fire out, deluge the place with water and cover it with dry earth. Be careful that none of the charred and unburned sticks retain any fire.

BRINGING HOME THE CATCH.

Not only for the sake of beauty do this, but also for the sake of the settlers and the lumbermen, whose "all" may be lost by your carelessness, for sometimes a small camp-fire fanned by the winds will run for miles and destroy a whole forest.

The streams falling into this lake are interspersed with rapids and waterfalls which form home and harbour for many speckled trout. It is somewhat peculiar to note that this class of fish seems to be almost restricted in this section to the neighbourhood of this lake, and running often up to three or four pounds weight. White fish and salmon trout are found in the lake itself. *Hollow*, *Fletcher* and *Hardwood Lakes* are all on the eastern branch of the main lake and noted for their trout. Under the name of *Trading Lake*, these waters have attained renown, and this name is still retained at the eastern extremity. A little further to the east is a lake whose name may be managed by those who have survived the little stream north of the Severn—*Lake Kahweambetewayamog*.

Captain Huckin's steamers *Dean* and *Excelsior*, the latter a capital new one of seventy-five feet keel, keep up the communications between Baysville and the post-offices and settlements around the lake.

At North East Bay, near *Dwight* Post-office, the continuation of the river enters the lake. Upon its waters are strung out a long series of little lakes, all affording good sport, among them *Ochtwan* (or Ox Tongue), *Canoe*, *Island*, *Big Joe* and other lakes By this chain there is a canoe route which has been already followed by several parties which, arriving at the head waters of the Muskoka, make a short portage to the *Petewawa* and *Madawaska Rivers*, thence down to the *Ottawa River*,—a round trip of much attractiveness and variety. *Go die's Hotel* at Dwight, will make a good headquarters—and a ready welcome be assured to all good sportsmen.

The district around Lake of Bays is most highly esteemed for its deer hunting, the best of duck and partridge shooting,—indeed, whether for rod or gun the visitor is sure of ample employment. Hereabouts are to be found " The happy hunting grounds of the Dwight-Wiman Sporting Club." Their names have become localized, and here for rest and recreation, zest and fresh energy comes annually that ardent Canadian, Erastus Wiman, whose successes in the United States seem only to intensify his affection for his native land. A good example gives he to the young Canadian.

From Goldie's, a line of excellent lakes run north, all full of sport, *Cooper*, *Devil's Angle*, *Long*, *Little Twin*, *Big Twin*, *Crotch*, *Poverty*, *Buck* and *Clear*, all communicating by short portages.

Good sport, canoes and guides who know where the best fishing spots are, and trained dogs accustomed to the vicinity for hunting, are all necessary. The names of the best men, well-known and reliable from having already conducted fishing and hunting parties through this district, are given in the list of guides.

Mr. W. H. Brown, of Baysville, is also referred to as an obliging correspondent.

The Maganetewan River Chain.

Leaving Huntsville, the railway crosses the Muskoka river near *Melissa* (39 miles), and then surmounts the water shed, during which several streams are followed, and the acute eye will note when those that run south are left and those that run north are met.

Katrine (55 miles), Morton's Hotel.—This is the centre of a splendid lake country. *Sand, Beaver,* and *Long Lakes,* on the South *Maganetewan River, Three Mile* and *Doe Lakes* close by. Here, as noted previously, connection is made with the Maganetewan River, and canoes or light boats can be taken for the water trip to Huntsville. The railway continues following the banks for four miles, during which the river is crossed four times, the next station is

Burk's Falls (60 miles).—This station opens up another and entirely new region to steamboat navigation to the tourist and the traveller, and particularly to the sportsman, who can now get with comparatively little trouble to a district which has hitherto been accessible only to those with ample means and time. This chain of lakes and the Maganetewan River is just equidistant between the Muskoka and Nipissing chains of waters, and drains a surface of about 4,000 square miles. Some idea may therefore be gathered of its magnitude, and of the possibilities for canoeing, opened up by the ramification of the numerous tributaries and their attendant lake enlargements.

The very heart centre for sport for rod and gun, its rivers and lakes can be ascended and descended in canoes and boats amid the best of sport, while the eye is fascinated by the fresh, unsullied wildness of its forest haunts. Wild birds and deer abound. Speckled trout are caught weighing 3 to 5 lbs.; bass, 5 to 8 lbs.; pickerel, 8 to 14 lbs.

" Music," in *Forest and Stream*, thus speaks of the Maganetewan : " Now a word about the region. If a man can stand out-door life, and live on venison, trout, bass, partridges, ducks, pork, tea and crackers, there is no better place to go to in America that is as accessible. A man can go there in July, August, September, or Octo-

THE NORTHERN LAKES OF CANADA.

ber with comfort, if he will go in the right way, and shoot deer and catch trout to his heart's content. June to August for trout, after that for deer. Remember the Maganetewan is as large as the Schuylkill at Philadelphia, or considerably wider and deeper than the Harlem at High Bridge, and that the trout have an unlimited range, and are

THE HUNTER'S CAMP.

seldom disturbed, so that they have a chance to grow. Deer can be bagged in great numbers if you choose to do so ; with a couple of good hounds magnificent sport could be had in the fall. I have shot partridges with my rifle from the canoe while travelling, as they were strutting on the shore, and their 'drumming' was one of the plea-

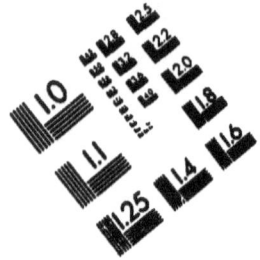

**IMAGE EVALUATION
TEST TARGET (MT-3)**

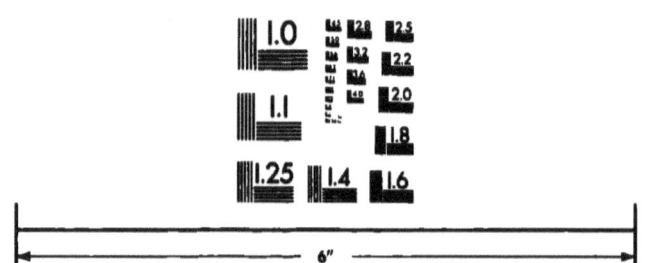

Photographic
Sciences
Corporation

23 WEST MAIN STREET
WEBSTER, N.Y. 14580
(716) 872-4503

santest every-day sounds. Do not try to go without some guide. There are men who know the country, and they should be secured, for if you get in there alone, you will have little sport and much trouble. I have no possible interest in noticing this region except that I believe it to be unsurpassed in many ways."

The village of Burk's Falls stands upon the banks of the main Maganetewan ("the smooth flowing water"), at the head of steamboat navigation, and about half a mile below the forks of the river where the two great north and south branches join. The station is half a mile from the town, in which are several good stores and three

LAKE AH-MIC.

country hotels—D. F. Burk's, Trimmer's, and the Cataract House, by W. F. Thomson. From here can be taken daily the new combined paddle and screw steamer *Wenonah*, of the Muskoka Navigation Company.

For fifteen miles the river is followed, winding to and fro, as all Muskoka rivers seem to do. *Lake Se-see-be* forms the next link for ten miles, at the foot of which is the thriving town of *Maganetewan*. Here the Great Northern Colonization road crosses the river and a centre for the surrounding districts has been formed. There are two hotels, Maganetewan House, by S. B. Fish ; Northern House, by Mr. Carroll. A number of stores form a particularly good headquarters during the hunting season.

After passing through the locks, the steamer continues for three miles more in the river, and then enters the lovely *Lake Ah-Mic.* This is another of the gems of Muskoka ; most quaint in form, its arms and elongations form a very maze of interlacings, so their constant vistas of projecting heights with glimpses of distant waters and high ridges with closely-wooded forests of hard wood trees, give soft rounded outlines to the distant scenery.

In summer this combination of the rich greens of the maple, oak and birch, is most beautiful, but when in autumn the bright red tints show forth their resplendent colours, it is simply indescribable.

The lake is twelve miles in length, and calling places are not yet very numerous. The Depot Farm, now called *Port Anson*, Thomas Baldock's Hotel, and *Ah-Mic Harbour* with Croswell's Hotel may be mentioned as attractive points where travellers will find very fair accommodation, at the end of his forty mile trip from the railway station.

This is also another excellent route for boating, as there are no rapids to interfere or portages to make while a nice diversity of paddling or rowing in the rivers is interspersed with sailing on the lakes.

The camping facilities are good, and not a few farm houses will give ready supplies and shelter. The pioneers who have penetrated to this country and settled on its lake shores are all sportsmen, and boats and canoes and skilful guides, whose wood craft has been learned by long practice on their own account, can be found everywhere.

From here on, the more adventurous can continue their canoe route by the Great River, twelve miles to *Lake Wah-wa-kesh*, and thence to *Byng Inlet*, about fifty-five miles away on the shores of the Georgian Bay. In this distance there are 21 portages, of varying lengths, from one of some two miles, to most of only a few yards. Their combined length is about eight miles, leaving 42 miles of good canoeing water. It is a trip not to be attempted without first-class guides. These portages made there are few difficulties to be overcome, and in good hands these form only the sources of adventure for which the trip is undertaken.

The Seguin Chain.

Dunchurch, a village three and a half miles by road from Ah-Mic Lake, is on the shores of *Whitestone Lake*, another of the celebrated centres for sport in fin and fur. The herring fishing in the narrows is most excellent, and the hunting and shooting of the best.

From here return can be made in another direction by taking the colonization road, 9½ miles, to the village of *McKellar*, which is the centre of another lake system. Here the canoe can again be put in the water and following the *Seguin River* and its enlargements, *Lakes Manitowaba, Trout*, and *Mill*, can with facility arrive at *Parry Sound*, on the shores of the Georgian Bay. There are only three portages in the whole distance, one of half a mile, and two of one mile each; there are also three very short lifts. The other following the eastern arm of *Lake Manitowaba* portage 2½ miles to *Blackwater Lake*, and then canoe through the connecting *Lake Isabella* past the village of Edgington into *Maple Lake* and *Marsh* and *Star Lakes*, and so portage again half a mile to Turtle P. O. on *Turtle Lake*, close to Port Cockburn on *Lake Joseph*.

Neither of these routes present very great difficulties, as they are almost entirely lake work.

These samples give some idea of the possibilities of navigation in the many connecting waters of the *Muskoka District*, and what a wealth of exercise and adventure lies before the youth of Canada.

The French River Chain.

Sundridge (70 miles), the next point of any importance, is on the shores of *Stony Lake*, the summit water of the south slope of the district being 268 feet above Lake Muskoka. The lake is shallow, very regular in form, without any islands, and abounds in fish.

South River (77 miles) is the first crossing of the new watershed, where the waters run north to Lake Nipissing. It is the highest point on the railway, and the dividing line between the two watersheds, being 378 feet above Lake Muskoka, and 553 above Lake Nipissing. One must suppose that this is called the "South" River because it runs "north" on the same principle as that given by Pat concerning the different Irish jaunting cars, on one kind of which the passengers sit back to back with their feet over the wheels, and the other face to face with their feet inside the car. "Oh, I dunno at all, but I suppose they call it an outsyde kyar becase the whales is insyde, and it's an insyde kyar becase the whales is outsyde."

Mr. Holditch keeps the hotel, the "Ontario Height of Land House," and intends putting up an observation platform in Moose Park, from where eight lakes can be seen in a circle of five miles. The *Dunbars Falls* of the river are worthy a visit, being 150 feet high. The river itself is from 150 to 200 feet in width, and a good canoeing stream. It is 24 miles paddle to Lake Nipissing, during which some rapids, but not very fast, are passed. The speckled trout in the river are the largest and most plentiful anywhere this side of Nepigon, and in the hunting season moose are met as well as large numbers of the red deer. It will be noticed that for some little time the appearance of the country has changed and the land improved. All through this latter part of the railway, immigration is beginning, and fine fertile farms with soil as good and opportunities better than the frontier farms of thirty years ago, will here be carved out of the forest. A certain market to the lumberman, and now easy access to the front country will settle up the better parts of this district.

Barretts (92 miles), is the centre of a large and thriving settlement, and another unexcelled centre for brook trout fishing and for moose and deer hunting.

Commanda is fifteen miles west by road from here, or can also be most conveniently reached by the regular stages running daily from Maganetewan (see page 154). This section has been deservedly awarded the highest renown for the record of its sport. Being somewhat remote, but now brought into more convenient access, the banks of the streams and of the lakes are more completely in the state of nature than elsewhere, and for miles unbroken forest hems in the view. Following up the Great Nipissing Colonization road from Maganetewan, about halfway is

Meganoma.—[We have struck the trail]. Russell & Archer's hotel here is absolutely first-class, kept by good caterers and ardent sportsmen. This is the centre for *Eagle Lake*, *Many Island*, *Spring* and *Pickerel Lakes*, and *Distress River*,—all celebrated fishing and hunting spots and comprised in what is known as the *Commanda District*.

Rye is also a good centre. The stages stop for dinner at Wm. Park's hotel. At *Commanda* itself Carr's Temperance Hotel and Fitzgerald's are good stopping places. From here the *Commanda River* can be followed through *Commanda Lake* and *Restoul Lake* to *Chaudiere Falls*, near the shores of Lake Nipissing, than which no more pleasant or more sporting route exists. As all this neighbourhood is comparatively uninhabited, it is not advisable to attempt it without guides.

After *Powasing* (95 miles) a good spot for trout on the *Jenesse Creek*, we arrive at

Lake Nipissing.

Callender (108 miles), on South East bay, gives the first glimpse of the waters, being situated on a hill side sloping up from the bay. At present there about forty houses and three country hotels. Here the steamers touch for various parts of the lake. At the entrance to the bay is a very numerous group of islands, almost all of which have been taken up by residents of Hamilton.

La Vase (112 miles from Gravenhurst and 226 from Toronto) is the connecting point with the Canadian Pacific Railway and the all-rail route to Manitoba and the North-West.

The Earliest Route to the North-West.

The country we have now arrived at would at first thought seem to have been newly discovered, and to be now for the first time opened to the transport of the civilized traveller. Yet long before the advancing European colonist had penetrated to the shores of the Niagara, this route, up the Ottawa valley and along the shores of Lake Nipissing—the very line of the newly constructed Canadian Pacific Railway—had been traversed by many traders and travellers, and was their highway between Montreal and the Red River Country.

As we have been travelling North, crossing the various East and West routes, and seemingly passing from the older and front countries to the newer and more remote districts, we have really been meeting them in the reverse order of their development. When the whites first commenced to trade with the interior of the continent by the Gulf of the St. Lawrence, the first route that was opened up by them was this by Lake Nipissing. Next came the *portage* by the Humber, or Toronto River, and Lake Simcoe; and *lastly*, that by the Niagara.

It was not until 1669 that Père Gallinée, canoeing around the western shores of Lake Ontario, says : " We found a river, one-eighth of a league broad, and extremely rapid, forming the outlet of Lake Erie, and emptying into Lake Ontario. The depth of the river is at this place extraordinary, for, on sounding close by the shore, we found fifteen or sixteen fathoms of water. This outlet is forty leagues long, and has, from ten to twelve leagues above Lake Ontario, one of the finest cataracts in the world; for all the Indians of whom I have enquired about it say that the river falls at that place from a rock higher than the tallest pines—that is, about two hundred feet."

Then was the Niagara River first met by the whites; and not until

1678 did Father Hennepin, the first European to see those Falls, stand by the cataract of Niagara.

Yet sixty-three years before this, in 1615, before even the Pilgrim Fathers had landed on the shores of America, Champlain, the French Governor of Quebec, had advanced with a party of armed men and passed up the Ottawa to Lake Nipissing. He found the shores occupied by between 700 and 800 Indians, and after enjoying its "abundance of game," and describing its northern side as being "very pleasant, with fine meadows for the grazing of cattle, and many little streams discharging into the lake," he passed down the French River to the Lake of the Hurons.

Following him came the *Coureurs-des-bois*, the voyageurs and trappers of the Canadian "North-West" and "X. Y." fur companies, carrying over the rocky portages all the stores for themselves and the Hudson's Bay Company, at Fort William, and the packs of furs which sought this, for nearly a century the main route between the North-West and Tide-water. Early travellers have described its dangers and difficulties, and the many crosses erected along the route—memorials of brave men who had lost their lives in battling with the turbulent rapids of the stream, or with the many foes along its banks, of whom stories of valour, or of pathos and self-sacrifice, such as that of the gallant Cadieux, " voyageur, poête et guerrier," float down in history :

> " Seul en ces bois, que j'ai eu de soucis !
> Pensant toujours à mes si chers amis,
> Je demandais : Hélas ! sont-ils noyés?
> Les Iroquois les auraient-ils tués?
> —E. GAGNON, *Chansons Populaires du Canada.*

Along the shores, the summer tourist can in fancy picture the passing lines of heavy-laden canoes, and hear once more the gay-hearted voyageurs singing out their cheerful French *chansons*, while keeping time with dripping paddle to the stirring tune.

A la Claire Fontaine.

From Chansons Populaires du Canada.—MORGAN, QUEBEC.

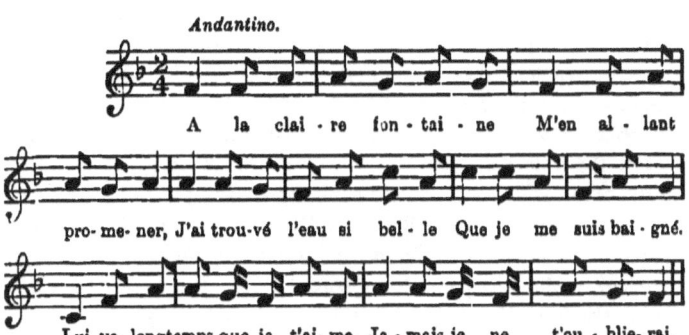

A la clai-re fon-tai-ne M'en al-lant
pro-me-ner, J'ai trou-vé l'eau si bel-le Que je me suis bai-gné.
Lui ya longtemps que je t'ai-me, Ja-mais je ne t'ou-blie-rai.

J'ai trouvé l'eau si belle,
Que je m'y suis baigné ;
Sous les feuilles d'un chêne
Je me suis fait sécher.
  Lui ya longtemps, etc.

Sous les feuilles d'un chêne
Je me suis fait sécher ;
Sur la plus haute branche
Le rossignol chantait.
  Lui ya longtemps, etc.

Sur la plus haute branche
Le rossignol chantait,
Chante, rossignol, chante,
Toi qui as le cœur gai.
  Lui ya longtemps, etc.

Chante, rossignol, chante,
Toi qui as le cœur gai,
Tu as le cœur à rire,
Moi je l'ai-t-à-pleurer.
  Lui ya longtemps, etc.

Tu as le cœur à rire,
Moi je l'ai-t-à pleurer,
J'ai perdu ma maîtresse
Sans l'avoir mérité.
  Lui ya longtemps, etc.

J'ai perdu ma maîtresse
Sans l'avoir mérité,
Pour un bouquet de roses
Que je lui refusai.
  Lui ya longtemps, etc.

Pour un bouquet de roses
Que je lui refusai.
Je voudrais que la rose
Fût encore au rosier.
  Lui ya longtemps, etc.

Je voudrais que la rose
Fût encore au rosier,
Et moi et ma maîtresse
Dans les même amitiés.
  Lui ya longtemps, etc.

The Parry Island Archipelago.

The *Penetanguishene* branch, after leaving Allandale, follows tl curve of the hills to the east of the *Nottawasaga Valley*. The riv is filled with the accumulations of the débris of the freshets of hu dreds of years, so that large portions of the valley are complete flooded in the early spring. Little by little it is being reclaimec but vast acres of forest still occupy the bottom banks ; and to tl left of the train a view is had over their waving tops, surging like green ocean with the inequalities of the surface.

Penetanguishene (102 miles from Toronto) is one of the histor spots of Canada, but in the impatient haste of these modern days has had to allow its name to be curtailed to " Penetang." The tov lies at the head of a deep inlet on the south-east shore of the Georgi: Bay, which early attracted attention as a safe and commodious h: bour. The importance of the naval command of the Upper Gre Lakes led the British Government, in 1818, to fix upon a site ne the mouth of the bay for the establishment of a dockyard. A w: sloop, the *Midas*, was here stationed for some years ; but the id of making a naval centre was shortly after abandoned. [The positi has since been occupied by a Juvenile Reformatory, maintained the Canadian Government]. The British Government had induc a number of pensioners to occupy lands in the vicinity which form part of the military reservation—the records of the names of ma of whom are to be found in the old Military Church, and under t waters of the bay may still be seen, on calm days, the sunken hu of the old gunboats of which they formed the crews.

The town, situated 2½ miles from the Reformatory, developec considerable trade in furs, large quantities of which were brought Indians and Half-breeds from the almost unbroken forests and cou less lakes to the North-East, which afforded an unrivalled hunti ground.

Some families of French and English Half-breeds and of French Canadians, who, on the giving up of Drummond Island, Lake Huron, to the Americans, in 1828, retained their British allegiance, were granted lands in the vicinity. In 1841 a number of their compatriots from Lower Canada joined them, forming what is now known as the French Settlement. In 1880 the census reports the French-speaking population of the County of Simcoe as 3,669, almost all of whom live within a few miles of Penetanguishene; and in the Roman Catholic churches the services are still rendered in the French language.

Pleasant excursions can be made from here to Midland City, Mouth of the Severn, Parry Sound, etc. The Clarkson House, on a height overlooking the bay, is recommended.

THE ARCHIPELAGO.

There are two lines of steamers which ply through these islands on the route to Parry Sound. The Great Northern Transit Company, from Collingwood, and the Parry Sound Company, from Penetang. Both lines of steamers pass through this maze of islands. Ten thousand have been counted about here in the nautical survey of the Georgian Bay, and the whole shore is fringed with them, of all sizes, from mere dots to hundreds of acres, with high towering cliff-like centres. Through the *Inside Channel* of these the steamers wind their way. One open spot only exists, *Moose Point*, where the lake has open sweep, but except this, all else is through channels, some so narrow as to almost touch the steamers' sides. Many of the Islands are occupied with summer-houses, and there is no doubt that ere long there will be as great a population as now takes its summer outings on the inland Lakes of Muskoka.

PARRY SOUND.

This large and flourishing town is beautifully situated at the mouth of the *Seguin River*, whose waterfalls are utilized for its gigantic sawmills, and upon a deep recessed harbour, completely sheltered from the open water. From it the summer can be spent either in exploring, by means of the several steam launches, the windings up the Archipelago, or striking inland, take the canoe trips up the interior. Good fishing abounds of the same character as inland, except that some extra-sized bass, old lake stagers, are occasionally captured.

The Belvidere Hotel ($1.50) is opened only in the summer season, being specially intended for tourists. Its situation upon a high hillside, facing the most beautiful view, has been excellently selected. The *Seguin House*, R. B. Armstrong, and *Albion House*, Henry Jukes

THE THREE SISTERS.

(both $1.00), are favourably mentioned. There are several churches, some good stores, a local weekly paper, and telegraph communication. It is just twelve hours' run, half boat and half rail, between Toronto and Parry Sound. Harvie's stage line runs regularly between here and Port Cockburn, Lake Joseph (24 miles). It is a good road, and passes along an almost consecutive line of pretty lakes. Round trip tickets, going one way and coming back the other, can be obtained, including both the Lakes of Muskoka and the Parry Island Archipelago.

The Hurons and French in the Early Days.

BY

MR. JAS. BAIN, JR., PUBLIC LIBRARIAN, TORONTO.

The early history of the existing town of Penetanguishene only carries us back to the beginning of this century, but the surrounding district recalls the history of a nation whose tragic fate was the theme of innumerable pens, and which disappeared altogether from the face of the country in the middle of the seventeenth century. At a time when the infant European settlements were struggling for bare existence in Salem, Fort Orange, Jamestown, and St. Augustine, French priests and traders, had worked their way up the turbulent rivers and through the trackless forests to this neighbourhood, and had organized an extensive mission and built a fort and church, the ruins of which exist to this day.

The Hurons, a branch of the great Huron-Iroquois family, had early separated themselves from their kindred, who were afterwards known as the Iroquois, or Five Nations, dwelling in what is now New York State. A bitter feud had arisen between them, and the warfare was conducted with all the cruelty and vindictiveness to be expected from the most ferocious Indians of this continent. The establishment of a fort at Quebec, in 1608, at once drew large numbers of the Hurons, to trade their furs for French goods. Their yearly visits attracted the attention of Champlain, the Governor of the new French possessions, who, as did Cartier when he named the first village above tide-water *La Chine*, still dreamt of reaching China and the golden East, and hoped to be able, with the Hurons' assistance, to gain the road to the Eastern seas. In 1615 he made his second attempt to reach their country, ascended the Ottawa River, crossing Lake Nipissing, and descending the river of that name, now called the French River, he gazed for the first time upon the great fresh-water sea of the Hurons.

Passing, in his canoe, along the eastern side of the Georgian Bay, threading his path amid the countless islands which line its shores, he finally landed at Thunder Bay, a few miles west of Penetanguishene. He was immediately taken to a town in the vicinity, called Carhagouthia, where he was welcomed by Father Le Caron, who had preceded him. On the 17th of August he reached the chief town, Cahiagué (near Coldwater).

The unfortunate decision which now led Champlain to join the Hurons in an attack upon the Iroquois, near Onondaga, was the immediate cause of the long and bitter warfare which almost resulted in driving the French from Canada. The expedition took its way by Balsam Lake, the Trent River, and the Bay of Quinté, thence across Lake Ontario. Having failed to carry the Indian fortifications in spite of the firearms of their French allies, they retreated to their homes. Champlain returned to Quebec in the following spring, after spending the winter in excursions through the Huron country. The number of towns and villages, he reported, was 32, and the population about 20,000; but a later traveller fixed it more accurately at 30,000. Well may Parkman say that "here, within an area of sixty or seventy miles, was the seat of one of the most remarkable savage communities of this continent." The entire population seems to have been confined to the country lying between the Georgian Bay and Lake Simcoe, with its northern extension, Lake Couchiching.

On the return of Champlain to Quebec, reinforcements were sent to the Mission; and as the annual *Relations* of the Jesuit Fathers were published in Paris, detailing the strange discoveries and painful labours of those who had ventured their lives, a fervent missionary spirit arose which was profitable to the Mission both in money and men. In 1639, the Jesuits, finding it imperative to establish some fixed headquarters, chose a spot on the banks of the River Wye, near where it empties into Matchedash Bay. Here they built a fort and church, named it Ste. Marie, manning the one with soldiers to the number of thirty, and adorning the other with the ecclesiastical ornaments which they had succeeded in transporting over the long reaches and weary portages of the Ottawa and Nipissing Rivers. The fort, built partly of stone, partly of wood, was enclosed within a palisaded fortification and surrounded by a moat. Within its gates, charity and medicines were dispensed to the poor and suffering from the surrounding Indian towns, and every means were adopted to lead the savage to the service of the church.

The Iroquois saw with intense hatred this settlement of white men to their north, and resolved to make a powerful effort to reduce the Hurons to subjection and to exterminate the French. A temporary peace which had been concluded between themselves and the French and their Indian allies was broken, and a series of desperate onslaughts was made upon the French settlements along the St. Lawrence, until almost the entire population was driven into the isolated forts for protection from the human wolves. Turning their attention next to the Hurons, a numerous party crossed Lake Ontario, and ascending the Humber River to its head waters, soon reached by bush paths their frontier town, at the foot of a range of hills, about twenty miles to the south-east of Penetanguishene, known as Teanaustayé or St. Joseph. The Hurons were caught unprepared; in a short time the town was in ashes and the inhabitants massacred, with the exception of 700 who were carried off prisoners. Father Daniel, the priest in charge, was cut to pieces in front of his own church. After destroying in a similar manner another small town in the vicinity, the Iroquois returned home in triumph. In 1649, eight months after, a larger party, principally composed of Senecas and Mohawks, said to number about 1,000, again crossed Lake Ontario, and leisurely hunting till they drew near to the Hurons, burst upon the settlements like a whirlwind, burning the towns and destroying the inhabitants, until the cowed remnant of the Hurons, clustered round the Fort of St. Marie, resolved to fly from their own country and take refuge in some of the islands to the north. The Jesuits had no option—if their flock fled they must accompany them, and accordingly the torch was applied to the buildings, and the result of years of labour was soon a mass of broken walls and heaps of ashes. Part of the stonework was standing about six feet above the ground as late as

1870, but has since been destroyed, and the mounds and hollows are are all that left of one of the earliest buildings of this continent.

A memorial church is being erected in Penetanguishene, to commemorate the martyrdom of the priests, Brebœuf and Lallemant, who fell victims to the ferocious cruelty of the Iroquois. The first resting place of the unfortunate Hurons was the Christian Island, lying ten miles to the North West, where the Jesuits once more erected a fort, of which the walls are still standing; but their spirit was broken, and harrassed again by the Iroquois, they scattered over the islands still further to the north, a small remnant alone remaining with the Jesuit fathers, and finally, when the surviving French left the country, accompanied them to Lower Canada, where in the little village of Lorrette, close by Quebec, their descendants dwell to this day. The towns of the Hurons were composed of long bark-covered houses, accommodating numerous families, easily constructed and as easily destroyed. Nothing was permanent, and the forests speedily overran their sites. With the one exception of Ste. Marie built by the French, we are dependent on the heaps of ashes, stone implements and burnt corn turned up by the settlers, for the identification of the dwelling places of a populous nation who passed away two centuries ago, leaving the country empty and desolate for almost an hundred years.

The Georgian Bay.

Reverting again to Allandale (page 81), the *Collingwood Branch* leads north-westerly over the level known as the "Pine Plains," once covered with stately pines, but now being rapidly changed to broad acres of grain-laden fields and meadow pastures. Passing *Angus* and crossing the *Mad* and *Nottawasaga Rivers*, a reminiscence of the olden days is preserved in the name of *Batteaux*, where the voyageurs used to embark their laden canoes, and then we reach the lake.

Collingwood. Forty years ago the shores were lined with forest, and the *Hen and Chickens* harbour was but the resort of the Indians, or the home of the wild fowl. Now a stirring town of 5,000 inhabitants occupies the spot. Sawmills and huge grain elevators meet the eye, and busy steamers connecting with all the upper lakes lie at the docks. There is good brook trout fishing in the neighbourhood, and pleasant excursions can be made to the *Caves*, in whose recesses the ice of winter lingers the summer through, or to the *Nottawasaga Beach*, where for miles an excellent drive can be enjoyed on the firm hard sands around the curving shore of the bay. Near the mouth of the river lies the skeleton hulk of an old British gunboat, driven hard upon the shore, and behind which, in the sand banks, have been found some of the round shot fired at it by the pursuers when it sought shelter from the foe.

Collins' "Grand Central Hotel," and Rowland's "Globe Hotel," can be recommended as excellent headquarters. (*See adv.*)

Leaving Collingwood by the Lake Superior or the Georgian Bay Line steamers, the *Blue Mountains* rise high above the town, and fringe the southern shores of the Georgian Bay. This is the same elevation which, running south-easterly across the peninsula, is successively known sixty miles inland, as the *Caledon Mountains*, at Burlington Bay as "The Mountain" and terminates in the "Niagara Escarpment," on the banks of the Niagara River. The *Christian Islands* lie out to the right, another *Nottawasaga Island*, with revolving lighthouse, nearer to the shore.

Meaford lies at the foot of a bay under the protection of the promontory of *Cape Rich*. A rich agricultural country lies at the back, drained by the *Bighead* and *Beaver Rivers*, in whose upper reaches good sport is still to be had in speckled trout. Pretty drives up there, and the *Cuckoo Valley*, and good boating and bathing on the shores of the bay make the little village a pleasant summer resort. Mrs. Paul's hotel has long been a favourite with city visitors, and Noble's hotel is also recommended. The district is celebrated for its fruit, particularly plums, which grow to a size and luxuriance not approached in any other part of Ontario. It is a strange fact, too, that under the shelter of the lofty headlands peaches and grapes grow freely in the open air.

Owen Sound, the next calling place, is around Cape Rich, and at the head of a deeply-recessed bay. It is the terminus in this direction of the Owen Sound division of the Canadian Pacific Railway which connects with Toronto, and is the starting point of their line of swift steel steamships plying between here and Port Arthur.

Ingles and *Engenia Falls*, and the river Sydenham, are picturesquely situated in the deep rock-bound valley. The town is fast advancing in importance, and is the centre of an improving trade.

From here the steamers take the direct course up the bay. *Lonely Island* marks almost half the way, and in the morning the northern shores, with the lofty granite cliffs of the *La Cloche Mountains* come into view. At their foot lies the sheltered channel on which is *Killarney*, a fishing village of much fish importance, originally called, in the Indian tongue, *She-ba-wa-na-ning* (here is a channel). It has been modernized in name, but the beauty of its surroundings still remains the same.

The Great North Manitoulin Channel.

From here begins the wonderously beautiful trip of the *Great North Channel* in behind the warding shelter of the *Great Manitoulin Island*. The steamers of the *Great Northern Transit Company* are really excellent models of what excursion and safe lake-going steamers should be. Carrying Her Majesty's mails, they call from little hamlet to hamlet along the Island shores, running into out-of-the-way recesses, and passing backwards and forwards to cross the North Channel in doing their "Local" business on a way that is entirely different to that of the direct routes of the "Through" steamers. The searchers for the novelties of this route are fast increasing in numbers, and its and the steamers' good name becoming proverbial.

A correspondent in the *Forest and Stream* thus describes the scene: "Islands succeed islands in an unbroken continuity hour after hour as we glide on ; islands of every conceivable size and shape, more numerous than the Thousand Islands of the St. Lawrence many times multiplied ; islands barren, wooded, sandy, rocky, columnar, gracefully rounded, precipitous and gently sloping, wind-swept and storm-polished, large, diminutive, and infinitesimal ; reefs widely spreading, and submarine monoliths whose peaks barely project above the surface. There is a breadth and sweep and never-ending change in the panorama which is all-absorbing to a mind intent upon the picture. For one hundred and seventy miles we steam through this island scenery ! In the calm repose of a summer's morning, when the waves are stilled and the face of the lake gleams like polished glass, the shadows fall heavily from the indented shores, and every rock and

tree is sharply outlined and reproduced inverted in the mirror. Then we seem to float on airy nothing, looking upward into cloudland and downward into cloudland, into depths above and below that seem illimitable. There is very little animal life upon the Islands. The mainland is a continuous upheaval of bare Laurentian billows of granite that once were molten. There is but a scanty growth of trees. Sweeping blasts have scathed them and frequent fires blasted out their vitality. There are very few houses and but little cultivation. Occasionally a bark canoe glides from behind a point, and at intervals a solitary fisherman's hut is descried. Were it not for the gaunt white gulls that hover over our wake or keep vigil on the rocks, this would be a solitude.

"In places the flinty strata of rocks yield a mineral wealth sufficient to induce the sinking of a mining shaft, or the back country affords a supply of furs which necessitates the establishment of a trading post and depot. At these the steamboat touches, sometimes to take in wood, sometimes to land a passenger, and anon to discharge some freight."

Captain Bayfield, R.N., who compiled the nautical charts of these waters, states that 27,000 islands have been counted in the combined shores of the Georgian Bay and the North Channel.

After, *Manitowaning*, a rising settlement on the island, where are said to be some good trout streams (Quinn's and the Commercial Hotel); next on the route comes *Little Current*, another hamlet, and here a tide sets between the islands with a four-knot current. It is said the tide is caused by the wind, that it sets in whichever direction the wind is blowing at the time. Still further on is the picturesque Hudson's Bay Company post, called *La Cloche*, with its sunny white buildings, red-roofed.

Gore Bay, one of the most important points upon Manitoulin Island, and the principal port to the free grant lands, is next touched at.

Crossing back again,

Spanish River, an important lumbering centre, is met, and from here the steamer, after passing through the narrow straits of the "Devil's Gap," threads its way through the islands that fringe the Northern shore.

Algoma Mills is the point where the Canadian Pacific branch, after leavi ϛ the main line and skirting the north shores of Lake Nipissing first approaches the waters of Lake Huron on its way to Sault Ste. Marie.

Blind River and *Missasaga River* empty the waters of the North water shed, and are connecting routes to the Indian reservation further inland. At *Thessalon* is Jackson's hotel, and boats and guides can be obtained for the upper trout streams of the Missasaga River.

The Direct steamers from Collingwood coming in through the Missasaga channel now join the route of the Local steamers, and at the *Bruce Mines*, 307 miles from Collingwood, are the huge chimney stacks and shops and piles of copper ore, and ranges of hovels two miles long that belonged to the great company that used to delve the precious metal from the bowels of the surrounding earth. The works have cost over a quarter of a million of dollars. After a particularly beautiful part of the route, in which the steamers wind through a series of small islands and so close to the cliffs in passing through the "Wilsons Channel,'" that a biscuit can almost be pitched to land, *Bear Lake* is next passed, and after the Nebeesh Rapids we presently enter the serpentine *St. Mary's River*, with its Indian

reservation and villages upon the Canadian side, and an occasional farm on the Michigan shore.

At the mouth of the *Garden River* are the churches of the Anglican and Roman Catholic missions to the Indians in this district.

Forty miles from Bruce Mines, we reach *Sault Ste. Marie*, with its foaming rapids, its great ship canal, and the rival villages that confront each other from either shore. Here, if one elects to tarry, he will find good fishing in the rapids and smaller streams in the vicinity. There are numerous Indians on hand to lend their services and canoes, and if the sportsman will try the Garden River, on the Canada side, he can fill his creel with trout. Sixteen miles below the Sault is Hay Lake and its outlets, affording fine trouting and good duck shooting in their respective seasons. There is a very comfortable hotel at Sault Ste. Marie, on the American side, called the

Chippewa House. In Fort Brady is a detachment of the United States regular army. The Canadian side is more picturesque, and there are some fine private residences there. Millar's and Murray' hotels are excellently kept and nicely situated on the banks of the river.

The waters of Lake Superior here pour over the *Sault Ste. Marie Falls.* There is no one bold single fall, but a continuous rapid of about three-quarters of a mile in length, the waters rushing down with great fury, and breaking in huge waves over the rocks.

SAULT ST. MARIE FALLS.

At the Sault is the seat of the Anglican Bishop of Algoma, and the "Shingwauk Home," a school for the education of Indian children. On the American side is the great ship canal with two sets of locks. The earliest built in 1855 are 70 feet wide and 350 feet long, and fine examples of masonry, but they have been far eclipsed by the new lock 80 feet wide and 560 feet long, which is perhaps as large as any lock in the world, and raises the vessels by one lift of 1 feet to the level of Lake Superior.

Tourists can stop over and go on by the next steamers, and enjoy some fishing or "run the rapids;" canoes and two men can be hired at fifty cents for each person. The white-fish of the Sault are the finest and firmest of the lakes. It is interesting to watch the Indians as, poling their canoes up the surging rapids, they peer through the clear waters to discover the fish swimming in the channels in the rocks, when suddenly dropping down with the swift current, they sweep them out with their long-handled scoop nets.

Mackinac.

Connection with this famed resort, where the United States Government has created the whole island a "national park," is made daily from Sault Ste. Marie by various lines of steamers.

On the special "Mackinac Excursions," the Collingwood steamers turn westwards at *St. Joseph's Island*, skirting the shores of *Drummond Island*, from which, at the time of its cession to the United States, the patriotic British population migrated to Penetanguishene. The St. Mary's river is the highway for an immense volume of trade, and many huge steamers and tows of barges laden with grain or iron and copper ore will be met with in its channels. At *Detour* entry is made from it into Lake Huron, and after running westwards the heights of *Mackinac Island* come into view.

Around this island centre many historic events. As *Michilimackinac* it appears in the early annals as one of the most coveted strategic points and was in succession held by all the nationalities who in successive ages warred for the possession of the internal communications of this continent. The many local guide books and the several "Histories of Mackinac" will tell the details. A fort tops the sheer precipice, at the foot of which lies a part of the town, and for picturesqueness of position can very rarely be equalled.

In 1761 the British had built the first old Fort Michilimackinac but in 1763 it was surprised by the Indians under the great chief, *Pontiac*, and the garrison almost wholly massacred. In 1764 the present *Fort Mackinac* was built, and upon its being given over to the United States in 1793, at the conclusion of the revolutionary war, the British removed their headquarters to a new fort erected about 40 miles to the north on St. Joseph's Island, some remnants of which still remain.

When the war of 1812 began, Capt. Roberts, who was in command at *Fort St. Joseph*, under instructions received from General Brock, sallied forth, with the gallant Toussaint Pothier (afterwards member of the Upper House of Parliament, Montreal) and 455 Canadians and Indians. Having dropped down the river in boats and canoes they landed on the north side of the Island at a place now called "English Landing," and re-took Fort Mackinac from the Americans.

In 1814, a force of United States troops of 1,000 men, under Col. Crogan undertook to recapture the fort but they were met at the *Dousman Farm* and repulsed with considerable loss, Major Holmes, the second in command, being killed, and having retired hastily to the shore they re-embarked on their vessels and sailed off the same evening.

Fort St. George was erected on the highest part of the Island by the the Canadians, who held possession of the place until 1815, when the island was peaceably surrendered to the United States, and the the name of the Fort was then changed to *Fort Holmes*, in honor of the Major who had been killed the previous year.

Visits can be made to "The Lovers' Leap, Arch Rock, the several battle fields, etc., and their legendary and historic lore sought out with pleasure. Summer hotels of the finest description, and palatial lines of steamers from Detroit and Chicago have combined to form this one of the most engaging summer resorts in the north, and from it radiate many series of connections, including this along the Great North Manitoulin Channel to Collingwood, or to the Northern Shores of the mighty Lake Superior. The round trip from Collingwood to Sault Ste. Marie and Mackinac occupies just about one week. From Mackinac or the Sault to Lake Superior about the same.

The North Shore of Lake Superior.

Through the Sault and into Lake Superior! We have traversed one vast Mediterranean, and another is before us.

Lake Superior is 460 miles long, 170 miles broad ; its depth is 800 feet, being 200 feet below the level of the Atlantic.

It is only now that we begin to realize the immensity of these inland seas. The voyage for duration is like a journey to Europe. Great ships of thousands of tons burthen, traverse its highways, and storms that are not surpassed in violence sometimes agitate its depths, but in the summer time its clear cold waters are seldom stirred except by passing thunder showers.

The direct steamers, after passing up the river from Sault Ste. Marie across *Waiska Bay*, now phonetically and modernly called Whiskey Bay, and by the noble headlands of *Iroquois* and *Gros Cap*, " the portals of Lake Superior," head directly across the lake.

The coasting steamer turns northwards and proceeding one hundred miles, after losing sight of land, arrives at *Michipicoton Island* and river. Here in summer the boats tarry a few hours that excursionists may pick up agates along the pebbly shore or catch huge trout in the adjacent waters. Were it not that larger fish can be taken on the Nepigon, the size and quantity of these would seem amazing. Some of the agates found here are of unusual beauty and transparency. The light-house keeper, who has a sort of monopoly of the business, in that he has thoroughly raked the placers, will sell a pint of them for about a dollar.

Hence to Port Arthur and Fort William, the distance is 306 miles. The cliffs around the North Shore are bluff to the water's edge. Among the *Slate Islands* is some very fine fishing, and large exports of salmon trout are made from here. All around this shore there are regularly established "fisheries" and the boats of the hardy fishermen may often be met with.

On the north shore of Lake Superior is the noble Nepigon Bay. Entrance is by the straits between lofty islands and cliffs 1,500 feet

L

from base to summit, ragged with shattered rocks or clad with verdure, or past small islets barely holding ground for a few small trees. At the mouth of the river is the famed Red Rock, sacred to the Manitou, and carved with hieroglyphics, the marks and relics of early Indian visits.

Of this rock, from time immemorial, has the Indian "Calumet" or pipe of peace been made, and far down upon the Mississippi, and in Mexico, in the mounds or tumuli of extinct races, are found samples of its peculiar stone.

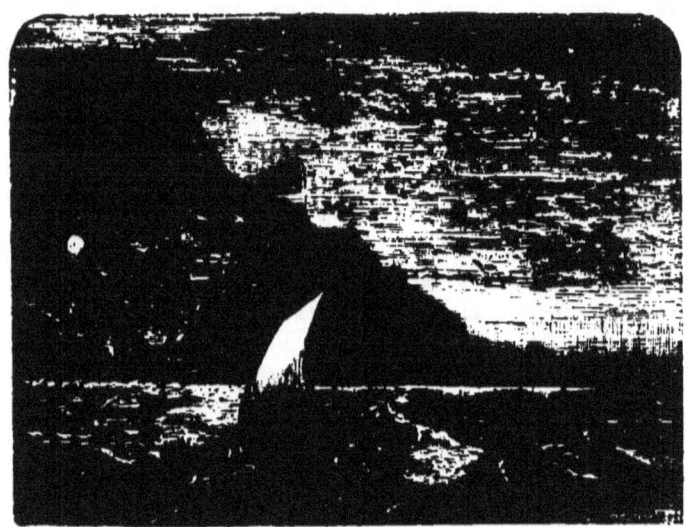

Half a mile from the mouth is the Hudson's Bay post.

Around the shores of *St. Ignace Island*, which divides the bay from the open lake, is magnificent lake trout fishing, (see Orvis Cheney "Fishing with the Fly") and the sport on the river is renowned.

Silver Islet lies under the shadow of Thunder Cape, and from its depths have been extracted many millions in value of silver, but now the mines, which were centred on a small rock barely above water,

THE NORTHERN LAKES OF CANADA.   179

have becom too difficult for profitable working, and attention is being directed to the main-land.

Thunder Bay, the great point of interest of the route is now entered, a grand expanse of water twenty miles in diameter, encircled by an amphitheatre of fantastic hills and guarded at its portal by Thunder Cape, a rugged headland of columnar basaltic trap of 1,350 feet high. When the steamer's whistle sounds, the reverberations

THUNDER CAPE—LAKE SUPERIOR.

leap and re-echo from point to point of the entire circumference of the bay. But when the Titanic voice of the thunder-blast rolls through the broad expanse, it resounds with mighty intonations that shake the cliffs and split the air, and give to cape and bay their most appropriate name. It is the tongue of the Great Spirit, Nana-bijoo, that speaks. And the god himself lies prone upon his back, like some ancient crusader resting from his labours. Looking from the distance his gigantic form can be seen plainly limned in the outline of the adjacent mountain ridge. It has been the custom of the ancient Indians to toss him a bit of tobacco, by way of a propitiatory offering, as they pass ! To the south-west is seen McKay's Mountain, and further to the left the peculiarly shaped Pie Island, its form resembling a gigantic pork pie.

Port Arthur.—Here is the Lake terminus of the Canadian National Highway, the Canadian Pacific Railway, which from here spans the Continent over forest, plain, and mountain range, to the temperate climate of British Columbia and the shores of the Pacific. Here too toward the east joins the just finished portion of the railway which, skirting the north shore of Lake Superior, running for miles around the bays and headlands in sight of the mighty waters, leaves them in the neighbourhood of Jackfish Bay, and cuts across the inland country to the shores of Lake Nipissing.

One cannot help comparing the *first* route of communication, when in canoes forced slowly and with difficulty up the rapids, or painfully carried over rugged portages from Montreal, up the Ottawa, over Lake Nipissing, and down the French River to the Lake Huron; then coasting with carefulness the long weary miles of rock-bound shore past the Sault the voyageur arrived at Thunder Bay, with this, the *newest* connection, its palace cars and express trains sweeping on swift wheels over the *same* route, often within sight of the same spots, beside the same rapids of the rivers and along the same shores of the lakes !

Where can a greater contrast be found between the *Past* and the *Present*, or where a more vivid example of the overcoming of the obstacles of nature by the genius and energy of man !

Port Arthur is growing fast. Into the lap of this bay is being poured the business of half a continent, and with it must come the welfare of the neighbourhood.

The Northern Hotel, kept by F. S. Wiley, faces the full view of the Bay, and will be a pleasant place where meetings for the summer holidays can be arranged between families from the North-West and their members which may have remained behind in Eastern Canada.

A most pleasant excursion can be made by small tug up the Kaministiquia river to *Pointe à Muron*, a distance of 12 miles, to the head of navigation, from where a magnificent view of Thunder Bay and the mighty ranges which encircle it like an amphitheatre can be obtained. *Pigeon River*, the boundary between the United States and Canada, and having fine Falls ; *Current River*, with rushing rapids and silver mines ; *Amethyst Bay*, where the beautiful amethyst veins are found in abundance ; *Silver Harbour*, the silver mines, and the numerous trout streams, will all give plenty to do and to amuse during the stay.

M'KAY'S MOUNTAIN.

Fort William is reached either by road or by boat, a pull of about two miles, or by the Canada Pacific R. R.. It is about the oldest Hudson's Bay post on Lake Superior, on the banks of the Kaministiquia River, a sluggish stream, winding with many a turn at the foot of *McKay's Mountain*, named after one of the early residents at the Hudson's Bay post. The ascent, although somewhat difficult, is well worth making. Following an Indian trail for about four miles, the precipitous sides of the mountain are ascended and the summit reached, about 1,200 feet above the level of the lake. Directly beneath winds like a silver thread the *Kaministiquia River*, dividing where it flows into Thunder Bay, into many channels, justifying its name, which means in the original " many-mouthed stream."

Eastward across the bay, at the distance of 25 miles, rises the lofty wall of Thunder Cape and attendant ranges. Then Pie Islands, the Welcome Islands, and far beyond them out in the broad water is the *Isle Royale*, a portion of the United States, to the left the Pointe a Muron range, with the river winding through them and the course of the Canada Pacific Railway, stretching far away through miles of forest. Around the river mouth cluster the giant elevators and the black masses of coal heaped up on the docks for transport inland, and through the web-like interweaving of the tracks puff the yard-engines of the railway sorting out the products of the Great North-West. The front of the mountain is a sheer cliff of 300 feet high to the first ledge, and from its giddy height an unbroken view of all the country round for 50 miles delights the eye. There are some good hotels in the town.

THE KAKABEKAH FALLS.

The Kakabekah Falls, another of the great natural features, are now, that the railway is constructed, quite easy of access. Canoes and Indians are taken out by train to a point about six miles above the Falls. The river is then followed to within a short distance above the cataract when a portage is made around the Falls which exceed in height and present a striking general resemblance to those at Niagara.

Rejoining the canoes, a run down the rapids brings the party to the mouth of the river in from three to four hours.

From Port Arthur connection is made by steamer to *Duluth*, "The Zenith City of the unsalted seas," of all places the most written of and talked of in the United States. It is advantageously situated at the extreme head of Lake Superior, and by railway connection with the interior, will, without doubt, some day justitify the glorious prophecies which heralded its birth. Here the steamers commence the return trip, having been joined by tourists from Chicago, St. Paul, Manitoba, &c., and picking up any who have "stopped off" at Thunder Bay, return by the same route, as previously described.

Whether it be for the return trip from either Toronto, Port Arthur, or Duluth, or for the single trip in one direction, opportunity is given for what is, beyond all question, the *Cheapest, Most Invigorating* and *Grandest Trip* on the continent.

Here then we will cease, having conducted our tourist from the shores of the Niagara over all the intervening waters and to the many pleasant summer resorts on

THE NORTHERN LAKES OF CANADA.

ERRATA.

Page 38, line 24, for "one hundred and fifty" read "fifty."
Page 81, line 20, for "Huron" read "Ojibbeway."
Page 113, line 16, for "miles" read "hours."

Our Country.

Our Country ! 'Tis a glorious land !
   With broad arms stretched from shore to shore
The proud Pacific chafes her strand,
   She hears the dark Atlantic roar ;
And, nurtured on her ample breast,
   How many a goodly prospect lies
In Nature's wildest grandeur drest,
   Enamel'd with her loveliest dyes.

Rich prairies decked with flowers of gold,
   Like sunlit oceans roll afar ;
Broad lakes her azure heavens behold,
   Reflecting clear each trembling star ;
And mighty rivers, mountain-born,
   Go sweeping onward dark and deep
Through forests where the bounding fawn
   Beneath their sheltering branches leap.

Still may her flowers untrampled spring ;
   Her harvests wave, her cities rise ;
And e er, till Time shall fold his wings
   Remain Earth's loveliest paradise !

Hints as to Routes.

☞All information and tickets for these Northern Lakes Routes can be obtained from BARLOW CUMBERLAND, General Ticket Agent, 35 Yonge Street (American Hotel Block), Toronto.

Toronto is the starting point for all points of interest in the "Northern Lakes of Canada."

Tourists from the Eastward, Boston, New York, can come by the connecting lines to Buffalo or Suspension Bridge, and then to Lewiston and Niagara to Toronto, or by Grand Trunk R. R. from Montreal.

From Niagara Falls and Buffalo, New York Central and Michigan Central Railroads connect at Lewiston and Niagara with palace steamer "Chicora" daily to Toronto, or the Grand Trunk Railway can be taken round the head of Lake Ontario.

Passengers from Toronto can have five hours at the Falls and return to Toronto same evening.

Tourists going down the St. Lawrence should not fail to stop at least one day in Toronto.

The Lakes of Muskoka are within a few hours of Toronto by the Northern Railway. Excursion tickets, good for the season, are issued to Bracebridge, Rosseau, Joseph and Parry Sound, and are available to stop at Barrie or Orillia by making known to the conductor the intention to do so. Round trip tickets to Parry Sound can be obtained to go *via* Muskoka Lakes and return by Georgian Bay.

For a grand all-round summer tour, this route is unsurpassed. Buffalo, Niagara Falls, Toronto, Couchiching, Lakes of Muskoka, Collingwood; thence Collingwood Line Steamers *via* Georgian Bay, Gt. Northern Manitoulin Channel, Sault Ste. Marie, North Shore of Lake Superior, Thunder Bay, Duluth, thence by rail to St. Paul and Chicago, or by Lake Superior Transit Co. *via* South Shore of Lake Superior to Detroit and Buffalo, or return by Collingwood Line and Northern Railway to Toronto. The whole round trip to Lake Superior returning to Toronto occupies ten days.

The most beautiful and economical trip on the Northern Lakes is to Sault Ste. Marie and return by the Great Northern Transit Company's steamer, calling at all the inland ports and in midsummer running specially to "Picturesque Mackinac." The round trip occupies six days.

These are the only lines passing through the inside picturesque route of the Georgian Bay and North Manitoulin Channel, avoiding the open waters of Lake Huron, and passing in daylight the LA CLOCHE MOUNTAINS, and through Island Scenery unsurpassed by the Thousand Islands of the St. Lawrence.

NORTHERN LAKES LINES

BARLOW CUMBERLAND,
Passenger Agency, Toronto.

Northern and North-Western Railway.
The Ontario all-Rail connection to the North-West and to all the Sporting Districts of the North.

Collingwood Lake Superior Line.
Great North Channel, Sault Ste. Marie, Lake Superior, Thunder Bay, Nepigon, Duluth, Manitoba, Dakota.

Georgian Bay Line.
Great Northern Transit Co., Georgian Bay, Manitoulin Island, Sault Ste. Marie, French River, Mackinac, Parry Sound.

Northern Navigation Compy.
Lake Simcoe, Barrie, Orillia, Lake Couchiching.

Muskoka Navigation Compy.
Lakes Muskoka, Rosseau and Joseph, the Maganetewan River, Lake Nipissing.

Niagara Navigation Compy.
Toronto, Niagara, Lewiston, Buffalo, Niagara Falls, New York, Boston, Philadelphia, and all points East or South.

Royal Mail Line.
Lake Ontario, The Thousand Islands, White Mountains, Montreal, Quebec Saguenay, Gulf of St. Lawrence.

OCEAN LINES.

INMAN LINE—Queenstown, Liverpool. GUION LINE—Queenstown, Liverpool. NORTH GERMAN LLOYD—London, Cherbourg, Bremen. STATE LINE—Belfast, Glasgow. RED STAR LINE—Antwerp. The Continent.

☞ Ticket and Passenger arrangements made, Berths secured, for all the above Lines.

BARLOW CUMBERLAND, General Ticket Agent

GUIDES.

It is often true economy to engage the services of those whose local knowledge will most quickly bring the newcomer to the best places for engaging in the sport for which he seeks, and at all events they will lighten his labours and certainly add to his pleasures. In canoeing, dangers may often be avoided. In deer hunting there is absolute necessity, and at all times, in an unknown country, it is well to have with one a Guide

> ...... who knows the bush
> As the seaman knows the sea.

Men and boys to row may be engaged from $1.00 to $1.50 per day.

Experienced fishermen and huntsmen, including canoes, $2.00 per day; Hounds, 50c. per day. The various Hotel-keepers may be consulted. The following men have been locally recommended :

Lakes Rosseau and Joseph and Moon River Districts.

Thos. Webster, John Peters, Abraham Asa..................Rosseau P. O.
R. Holton..Ashdown "
Jas. Davis, Frank Wing......................................Trout Lake "
J. Jennings, H. Vankoughnet................................Folding "
Wm. Brady, John Richards.................................. Port Cockburn "
Ed. Yellowhead, Joe Ingersoll, Sampson Ingersoll, John Bigwin...Bala "

Lake of Bays and South Branch, Muskoka River District.

Dorset P. O.

Allan Phillips, Alvin Phillips, Henry Sawyer, Chris. Sawyer, Matthew McCaw, Tom Keown.

Dwight P. O.

Thos. E. Salmon, Archie Goldie, Edward Goldie, William Blackwell, Frank Blackwell, Arthur Osborne, Tom Salmon, George Robson, Grieves Robson, James Trueman, William Trueman.

Baysville P. O.

Daniel Vancliff, Henry Vancliff, Samuel Vancliff.

Menominee P. O.

Jeff. Avery, and his Sons.

Commanda District.

Thomas Grawbarger... Restoul P.'O.
Thomas Smith.........   "   "
Thomas Armstrong....Nipissing "
R. Manering............Rye "
Wm. Porter...........Restoul "
John Suttiffe..........Ardagh "

Nipissing District.

Nicholas Wessels..Buolah Creek P. O.
Fred. Killey......   "   "
Sam. Lett........   "   "
Jas. Sheppard........La Vase "
Rich. Jessup..........   "   "

Maganetewan District.

George Ross................................Spence P. O.
J. McMillan.............................Maganetewan "
Wm. Harris......."".............................   "   "
Jos. Jenkins...................................   "   "
John Wilkins........................Dunchurch "
John Labrash.......................Maple Island "
H. Armstrong........................McKellar "
S. G. Ritter..................................   "   "

Hints as to Camping Outfit.

The equipment carried by "Campers" varies according to their fancy. The following are the most necessary requirements:

EQUIPMENT.—Ridge Tent, No. 3. The pole can be carried from place to place, and pins and uprights cut on landing. For a larger party a smaller tent to shelter the "cook" and the provisions is desirable. Axe, hatchet, deep pot or bake kettle, sauce pan, frying pan, gridiron, kettle, tea-pot, long iron spoon, long iron fork, butcher knife, knives, forks, and spoons, tin wash dish, round tin dish pans, tin cups, tin, or thick earthenware plates, water pail, sugar, salt, pepper, and tea cans, two hand lanterns for candles.

PROVISIONS.—Biscuits, flour, bread, sides clear bacon sewn in canvas, tea, sugar, salt, pepper, soap in bars, condensed milk, raisins, beans, dried apples, rice, matches, sperm candles.

CLOTHING—One change of underclothing, flannel shirt, and woollen trousers; three or four pairs of wool socks, overcoat, or mackintosh, heavy long boots for day, pair easy old gaiter boots, or leather slippers for camp, extra cap or tuque, handy bag for small things, large dunnage bag to hold all clothing.

The Game Laws of Ontario.

The Game Laws of Ontario are rigidly enforced, particularly in the district of Muskoka, where the residents are fully alive to the fact that in the providing of good sport, both with gun and rod, lies opportunity for large cash earnings by their community from the visitors who come among them.

Game inspectors are appointed in each township, who are empowered to watch their neighbourhood, to inspect boxes or receptacles, and search houses, when they have reason to believe game, or skins of game, are concealed out of season, and to summon offenders before the justices of the peace.

Confiscation of the game follows conviction.

SEASONS FOR SPORT.

Fish and game *may be taken* within the following periods :

FISH:

Salmon and lake trout	1st Dec.	to 1st Nov.
Speckled or brook trout............	1st May	to 15th Sept.
Bass	15th June	to 15th May.
Maskinonge and Pickerel	15th May	to 15th April.

GAME.

Deer, elk, moose, reindeer, caribou..	15th Oct.	to 15th Dec.
Woodcock	15th Aug.	to 1st Jany.
Grouse, pheasants, prairie fowl, partridge.................................	1st Sept.	to 1st Jany.

Snipe, plover.......................... 1st Sept. to 1st Jany.
Swans or Geese......................... 1st Sept. to 1st May.
Duck and all other water fowl......... 1st Sept. to 1st Jany.
Hares .... 1st Sept. to 15th March.

Quail may not be taken at all during 1886, 1887, nor wild turkey during 1886, 1887, or 1888, and thereafter only from 15th October to 15th December.

No person may have any of above game in his possession except during the above stated periods, or for the purposes of being exposed for sale for fifteen days after such periods.

No eggs of game birds may be taken at any time.

No game may be taken by trapping, nor by use of swivel guns or sunken batteries, nor during the night from one hour after sundown to one hour before sunrise.

FUR BEARING ANIMALS.

No beaver, mink, muskrat, sable, martin, otter or fisher may be hunted or taken except between 1st November and 1st May, and any one finding any traps set for them during any other time, may destroy the traps without incurring any liability. No muskrat houses may be broken into at any time.

Where imported kind of game is preserved by any one "on their own lands," no one can hunt it without the consent of the owner of the land.

No hound or dog, known to pursue deer, shall be allowed to run at large from the 15th Nov. to the following 15th Oct.

No deer can be exported from Ontario.

FINES.

	Not less than	Not more than
In case of deer....................Each offence	$10	$50
In case of birds or eggs .... "	5	25
In case of fur trapping............. "	5	25
Other breaches................ "	5	25

Costs are payable in addition to fines. The whole fine goes to the inspector, or to the prosecutor if not an inspector.

List of Islands and Owners.

LAKE MUSKOKA.

Nos.	Name.	Owners.
1	Horse Shoe	Barker.
2	One Tree	
3		
4		
5	Wolesley	
6	Apollo	
7	Sappho	
8	Kewaydin	Mrs. Ross.
9	Hillerest	
10	Hiawatha	
11	Friday	
12	Seven }	
13	Sisters }	
14	Robinson Crusoe	
15	Crown	
18	Ship	
21	Gibraltar	Prof. Taverner.
25	Morris	
26	Shaw	
27		
28	Wunilah	
29		
30		
	Camp Comfort	
31		E. Morris.
32		J. H. Morris.
35	Columbia	Madame Janeck.
36	Murillo	
37	Home	H. C. Rodick.
38	Fairholm	W. E. Foot.
39	Duncan	
40	Marion's	
41		J. McNabb.
44	The Brothers	R. T. Pope
45		J. H. Morris.
46	Burnt	
47	Birch	
48	Frank	
49	Frank	
50	Eilian Gowan	
52	Chief	

THE NORTHERN LAKES OF CANADA.

LAKE MUSKOKA—(Continued.)

Nos.	Name.	Owners.
54	Browning's	
—		
—		
57	Walker's	
58		
59	Delamere	J. M. Delamere.
60		S. Denison.
61	Twin Bluffs	Wm. Millar.
62		
63	Island F.	R. K. Burgess.
64	Plumpudding	
65	Fishermans	
66	Beach Grove	T. E. Moberly.
67	Heydon	G. T. Denison.
68	Crawford's	
69	Rankin	
73	Gairney	
76	Broomleigh	
79	Whitt	
80	Ault-Dowrie	
83	Gull	
84	Katago	
92	Mary	
"	Daisy	
"	Henry	
"	Percy	

LAKE ROSSEAU.

Nos.	Name.	Owners.
1	Shady	J. Maclennan.
2		
3		H. Kingsmill.
6	Picnic	Jas. Maclennan.
7	McKeaggie	J. McKeaggie.
8		
9	Jaw Bone	
18		R. K. Burgess.
Point	Idleswood	Mrs. Little.
19		Rev. M. Sanson.
20	Carter	E. T. Carter.
21	Yorum	Mr. Murray.
22	Mazengah	C. E. Blachford.
22		H. P. Dwight.

THE NORTHERN LAKES OF CANADA.

LAKE ROSSEAU—(Continued).

Nos.	Name.	Owners.
23	Fairy Lands	G. C. Lilly.
24	Prospect	
25	Olive	Robt. Baldwin.
26	Beacon	Dr. Hall.
27	Cedar	C. S. Warren.
28	Oak	Dr. Hall.
—	Flora	Dr. Hall.
29	Goulding	G. Goulding.
Point	Eagle's Nest	J. C. Lilly.
30	Sunny Side	R. K. Burgess.
Point	Aurora	Mr. Beddoe.
31	Fair View	R. K. Burgess.
32	Edith	R. L. Gunn.
33	Violet	Capt. Ord.
34	Warsaw	do.
	Arthur	do
36	St. Leonard's	Hon. W. Cayley.
37	Red	Capt. Ord.
38	White	do.
39	Blue	do
40	Cassie	
41		H. Baker.
42	Bohemia	J. S. Ploskell.
43		K. Moysey.
44	Bakers	A. Baker.
45	Vacuna	Mr. Soadding.
46	Craster	J. W. Thomas.
48	Bass	J. P. Clark.
49	Caledonia	P. M. Shannon.
50	Florence	W. J. Florence.
51	Wellesley	J. E. Smith.
52	Silver	Mrs. Molesworth.
53	Norway	A. F. Macdonald.

LAKE JOSEPH.

Nos.	Name.	Owners.
1, 2	Summit House	H. Fraser
3	Round	Jas. Maclennan
4		do
Point	Burgess	R. K. Burgess.
5		Jas. Maclennan.

LAKE JOSEPH—(Continued.)

Nos.	Name.	Owners.
6	Emerald	Jas. Baine.
7	Wegausind	Jas. Maclennan.
8		
9	G	J. S. Playfair.
10	Gitchemene	W. B. McMurrich.
"	Harmony Hall	do
11		Prof. Campbell.
12	Waneshing	J. H. Morris.
13	Yoho	Prof. Campbell.
14		Jas. Maclennan.
15		do
18	Chief	J. H. Mason.
19	Strawberry	A. B. Lee.
20	Cliff	do
21	Baco	do
22	Eagle	do
23	Grebe	do
24	Loon	do
25	Lilbourne	W. S. Jackson.
26		Dr. G. F. Cameron.
27	Teaberry	A. B. Lee.
28	Governor's Island	Lieut.-Gov. Robinson.
29	Elsinore	W. R. Johnston.
31	Reef	
32	Badgerow	G. W. Badgerow.
33		Dr. Oldwright.
34	Nissowema	
35		
36	Rose	J. Rose.
37	Lount	G. Lount.
38	Wolverton	H. Wolverton.
39		Dr. Caniff.
Point	Haggart's	Mr. Haggart.
"	Wood's	S. C. Wood.
40	Sugar Loaf	H. Stowe.
41	Stratford	J. P. Woods.
42	Morrison	R. Morrison.
43	Fisher	J. Fisher.
44		
45	McFarlane	G. McFarlane.
46	Surveyors	
Point	Moss Rock Lodge	H. S. Crews.
"	Mount View	R. F. Smyth.
47	Scadding	Mr. Scadding.
51	Robinson	C. Robinson.
52		
53	Schooner	

LALE JOSEPH—(*Continued.*)

Nos.	Name.	Owners.
54	Perch	Dr. Hodgins.
55	Grant	J. Minto.
56	Bass	Dr. Hodgins.
57	Pickerel	do
Point	Redwood	Mrs. Ardagh.
58		E. Cox.
59	Stowe	Dr. Stowe.
Point		Dr. G. Wright.

THE CLIFTON HOUSE,

NIAGARA FALLS,

Is so situated on the bank of the river that from its windows and balconies a comprehensive view of the Great Cataract may be had. The view at night of the

American Falls Illumined by the Electric Light,

the varied hues of the falling waters, and the strange play of light of many colours upon the ever-rising foam, is grand beyond description. From no other first-class Hotel at Niagara can a view of the Falls and Electric Illumination be had.

IT IS SEEN ONLY FROM "THE CLIFTON."

The Cuisine and Service of The Clifton will be carefully maintained at the highest excellence, and no pains spared to make the stay of visitors pleasant and enjoyable.

PARLOURS AND ROOMS with Baths attached may be had en suite.

OMNIBUS FARE SAME AS TO AND FROM OTHER HOTELS AT NIAGARA.

Address,

G. M. COLBURN, Proprietor,

NIAGARA FALLS, N.Y.

INDEX TO CONTENTS.

	PAGE	
A Little Farther On	3	Banks
The Hudson River Route	6	St. James' Cathedral
The Delaware Valley Route	7	The Public Library
To and From the West	9	Metropolitan Church
Niagara Falls	12	St. Michael's Cathedral

The Niagara River.

The Normal School
The Picture Galleries

Along the American Side	15	"How Perseus brought back the Gorgon's head"
The "Gorge" of Niagara	17	

Queenston Heights.

Baptist Church.

Where the Falls once were	21	Horticultural Gardens
Speech of Justice Macaulay	22	Osgoode Hall
Speech of Sir John Robinson	23	The Parks
Brock's Monument	24	The Universities
The View from the Summit	25	University of Toronto
Along the Canadian Side	27	Knox College
Niagara-on-the-Lake	27	Trinity College
The Battle of Queenston Heights	29	Government House
The Death of Brock	31	Grand Opera House
		"Off for a real good Fish"

The Forts of Niagara.

The Northern Railway.

The Early Struggles	33	Height of Land
The French Occupation	34	Vale of Aurora
The British Occupation	36	Holland River
The Americans take Fort George	39	Bradford
The Canadians retake Ft. Ni'gara	40	
Map of Niagara River	41	*The Severn River Chain.*

Lake Ontario ... 42

Lake Simcoe

Toronto Island	44	Allandale
Toronto as a Summer Resort	45	Orillia
		Lake Couchiching

The City of Toronto.

Sparrow Lake
Kasheshebogamog

Name and Early History	47	Canoe Route to Waubaushene
King Street	50	
Yonge Street	51	From Niagara Falls *via Hamilton*.
Map of Toronto	53	Burlington Beach
Street Car Routes	54	The North Western R.R.
Drives	55	"My Little Girl's first Fish"

The Public Buildings.

The Lakes of Muskoka..

The First Railway	56	Water and Rocks
Custom House	57	

INDEX TO CONTENTS.

	PAGE		PAGE
Origin of Name	100	Mary Lake	146
Gravenhurst	101	Port Sydney	146

The Muskosh River Chain.

Canoe Route by South Branch.

Lake Muskoka	102	Peninsula Lake	147
The Muskoka River	105	Rocky Portage	148
Bracebridge	106	Lake of Bays	149
The Great South Falls	107	Baysville	149
Beaumaris	111	Camp Fires	150
A Specimen Muskoka Letter	114	Madawaska River	151
Bala	116	Erastus Wiman	151
The Muskosh River	116		
The Indian River	117		
Port Carling	118		

The Maganetawan River Chain.

Melissa	152
Katrine	152

Lake Rosseau	119	Burk's Falls	152
Windermere	121	Sport	153
Three Mile Lake	122	Lake Se-see-be	154
Skeleton River	123	Lake Ah. Mic	155
Port Rosseau	123	Lake Wah-wa-kesh	155
The Shadow River	125	Canoe Route to Byng Inlet	155
Maplehurst	126		
Venetia	128		

The Seguin River Chain.

Oaklands	129	Whitestone Lake	156
Ferndale	129	McKellar	156
Clevelands	131	Canoe Route to Parry Sound	156
Gregory	131	Canoe Route to Lake Joseph	156
Port Sandfield	132		

The French River Chain.

Lake Joseph	134	Sundridge	156
Joseph River	135	South River	157
Craigie Lea	136	Canoe Route to Lake Nipissing	157
Little Lake Joe	137	Commanda	158
Yo-ho-cu-ca-ba	137	Canoe Route to Restoul Lake	158
Port Cockburn	138	Meganoma	158
Echo Rocks	139		

Lake Nipissing.

Canoe Route to Parry Sound	140	Callender	158
Crane Lake	140	La Vase	158
The Moon River	141	The Earliest Route to the North-West	159

The New Railway.

Utterson	142	Champlain	160
Huntsville	142	Cadieux	160
		A la Claire Fontaine	161

The Muskoka River Chain.

The Parry Island Archipelago.

Canoe Route to the Headwaters	143	Penetanguishene	162
Lake Vernon	143	The Archipelago	163
Hoodstown	143	Parry Sound	164
Fox Lake	144	The Hurons and French in the Early Days	165
Axe Lake	144		
Doe Lake	145		

Canoe Route by North Branch.

The Georgian Bay.

| Fairy Lake | 146 | Collingwood | 168 |

INDEX TO CONTENTS.

	PAGE
Blue Mountains	169
Meaford	169
Owen Sound	170
The Great Manitoulin Channel.	
She-ba-wa-naning	170
Manitowaning	172
Algoma Mills	172
St. Mary's River	173
Sault Ste. Marie	174
Mackinac.	
The Island	175
Military History	176
The North Shore, Lake Superior.	
Michipicoten Island	177
Slate Island	177

	PAGE
Nepigon	178
Thunder Cape	169
Port Arthur	180
The Past and the Present	180
Fort William	181
Kakabekah Falls	182
Duluth	183
Our Country.	184
Hints as to Routes	185
" " Camping Outfit	188
Guides	188
The Game Laws	189
Names and Owners of Islands.	
Lake Muskoka	191
Lake Rosseau	191
Lake Joseph	193

INDEX TO ADVERTISEMENTS.

Transportation. PAGE.
Great Northern Transit Co. 205
Canada Transit Co. 204
Northern and North-Western R. R. 206
New York Central R. R. 203
Niagara Navigation Co. 202
Lehigh Valley R. R. 8
Hudson River Day Line 208
"   "   People's Line 208
Muskoka Navigation Co. 207
Steamer Southern Belle 7
Merchants Line 210
Sundries.
Rice, Lewis & Son, hardware iv
W. A. Bradshaw, grocer and ship goods. iv
J. Mallon & Co., butchers v
Geo. Verrall, cabs v
D. Pike, tents, etc. vi
D. Millman, photos vi
W. McDowell, fishing tackle vii
J. E. Ellis, jewellery viii
Fulton, Michie & Co., camping supplies 201
P. C. Allan, camp furniture 109
Aikenhead & Crombie, hardware and
    fishing tackle 100
Allcock, Laight & Co., fishing tackle .. 222
Woltz Bros., jewellery 200
Cox & Co., brokers 200
Chi a Hall, chinaware 201
W. Hanna & Co., general store 214
Jordan, general store 214
Thos. Walters, saw mill 214
J. S. Wallis, general store 215

PAGE.
F. D. Stubbs, grocer 215
Sewell Bros., tourists' supplies 210
Hotels.
NIAGARA FALLS—Clifton House 198
Niagara-on-the-Lake—Queen's Royal ... 2
TORONTO—American 223
"   Queen's ii
"   Revere 223
"   Rossin .... Back cover
"   Walker 3
Burlington Beach Hotel 7
MUSKOKA.
Beaumaris—Prowse Hotel 218
Port Carling—Vanderburgh House 213
"   Stratton House 213
"   Oakland Park Hotel 215
Windermere—Aitken Hotel 219
Rosseau—Monteith House 214
Ferndale—Penson Hotel 217
Clevelands—C. J. Minett 217
Maplehurst—Brown's Hotel 219
Port Sandfield—Prospect House 212
Craigielea—Craigielea House 214
Port Cockburn—Summit House 200
Ah-Mic Harbour—Croswell Hotel 214
Huntsville—Dominion Hotel 217
Baysville—Forest House 219
PARRY SOUND—Belvidere Hotel 216
COLLINGWOOD—Globe Hotel 220
"   Central Hotel 220
Meaford—Paul's Hotel 221
"   Noble's Hotel 121
PORT ARTHUR—The Northern Hotel 219

HEADQUARTERS
—FOR—
Tents, Camp-Furniture, Hammocks, &c., &c.

FOLDING CHAIRS AND STOOLS FOR STEAMBOATING IN GREAT VARIETY.

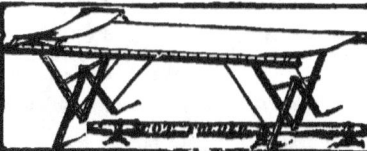

Just the thing for the lawn, verandah or "The coolest place in the house."

Price only $2.50.

The Champion Folding Camp-Cot opens and shuts like a Jack-knife, and will carry half a ton weight with perfect safety.

When not in use occupies no more space than a broom. Expressed to any addres on receipt of $2.50 or C. O. D. Write for complete illustrated catalogue of abov goods ; also of out-door games,

LAWN TENNIS, BASE BALL, CRICKET, LACROSSE,
&c., &c., to

P. C. ALLAN'S
City News and Games Depot,
35 KING STREET WEST, TORONTO.

AIKENHEAD & CROMBIE,
HARDWARE,
Corner King and Yonge Streets, Toronto,

—IMPORTERS OF—

Rodgers' Fine Pocket and Table Cutlery,

GALVANIZED BOAT and CANOE FITTINGS,

Cordage, Oakum, Blocks,

Fine Iron Stable Fittings and

Patent Magic Feed-Box.

Builders', Machinists', Carvers,' Blacksmiths' Supplies and every description of Hardware.

Fishing Tackle and Dog Collars in Great Variety.   Established 1830.

WOLTZ BROS. & CO.,
IMPORTERS AND DEALERS IN
DIAMONDS,

Fine Swiss and American Watches, Gold Chains, Ladies Gold and Silver Jewellery, Gold Headed Canes, Gold Thimbles, Sterling Silver and ELECTROPLATED WARE, etc., etc.

We would call sepcial attention to our fine adjusted Swiss Watches, Minute Repeaters, Sporting Watches, with independent split second; also single flyback attachments, fine OPEN face watches suitable for railroad conductors and engineers.

Every Watch Warranted to Give Satisfaction.

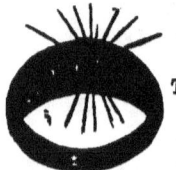

Our $20.00 Diamond Rings,

The best value in the market. Sent by mail on receipt of price.

WOLTZ BROS. & CO.,
29 King Street East, Toronto, Ont.

COX & CO.,
STOCK BROKERS,
(MEMBERS TORONTO STOCK EXCHANGE.)

Have the only Independent Direct Wire giving continuous New York Stock quotations, and which are received QUICKER THAN BY ANY OTHER LINE.

Buy and Sell on Commission for Cash or on Margin

ALL SECURITIES DEALT IN ON THE TORONTO, MONTREAL, AND NEW YORK STOCK EXCHANGES.

ALSO EXECUTE ORDERS ON THE

CHICAGO BOARD OF TRADE

In Grain and Provisions.

Daily Cable Quotations of Hudson's Bay and other stocks

26 TORONTO STREET.

CHINA HALL,
49 King St. East, Toronto.

One of Toronto's Greatest Attractions.

ITS ART ROOM ALWAYS FILLED WITH ORNAMENTS OF THE LATEST DESIGNS FROM THE BEST EUROPEAN MARKETS.

Dinner, Dessert, Tea and Breakfast Sets
In English and French China and Stone
PARIAN MARBLE,
Bisque and Bronze Figures and Ornaments,
ELECTRO-PLATE, LATEST NOVELTIES.
HOTEL GLASS, CHINA AND CUTLERY A SPECIALTY.

GLOVER HARRISON, Proprietor.

FULTON, MICHIE & CO.,
GROCERS,
WINE AND SPIRIT MERCHANTS,

are prepared to supply a full assortment of every requisite for

CAMPING, FISHING AND SHOOTING.

Soups, Meats and Vegetables,
Hams and Bacon, etc., etc.

ALL KINDS OF LIQUORS, TOBBACCO AND CIGARS.

Goods Packed Carefully and Promptly Delivered.

7 King Street West, Toronto.

SHORTEST ROUTE
BETWEEN
TORONTO
—AND—

ALL POINTS NORTH AND EAST IN ONTARIO

—AND—

NIAGARA FALLS, BUFFALO,

NEW YORK, BOSTON,

Philadelphia, Washington, Pittsburgh, Erie, Cleveland, Cincinnati, and all Points South of the Lakes.

NIAGARA NAVIGATION COMPANY

PALACE STEAMER

"CHICORA"

Leaves Yonge Street Wharf, Toronto, daily (except Sundays) at 7 a.m. and 2 p.m. for Niagara and Lewiston; coming north, leaves Lewiston (Eastern time) 10 a.m. and 5.30 p.m. and Niagara-on-the-Lake half an hour later, making close connections with the New York Central and Michigan Central Railways. Through Tickets to all points East and West. For tickets and all information, apply at office on steamer or to all agents on railways connecting with Buffalo.

BARLOW CUMBELAND,	JOHN FOY,
Ticket Agent, 35 Yonge St. TORONTO.	Manager, Toronto.

☞ **When going to the Thousand Islands or St. Lawrence Rapids, or to Niagara Falls, do not fail to see the Historic Niagara River.**

New York Central
—AND—
HUDSON RIVER RAILROAD.

THE FAVOURITE ROUTE FOR TOURISTS

Solid trains with luxurious PARLOUR and SLEEPING CARS from Suspension Bridge, Niagara Falls and Buffalo to

NEW YORK AND BOSTON.

THE NEW YORK CENTRAL affords its patrons the best accommodation and the finest scenery on the American Continent, embracing views *en route* of the

Niagara River and Falls, The Beautiful Mohawk Valley,

and the Picturesque and Historic Hudson.

● THE ONLY 4-TRACK RAILROAD IN THE WORLD ●

Having two tracks for freight traffic and two tracks exclusively for passenger business, thus ensuring **PERFECT SAFETY** and a certainty of arrival at destination **ON TIME**.

It is also the only line having a DEPOT IN NEW YORK CITY, thus saving its patrons the inconvenience of being transferred to another state by ferry boat.

For any information not obtainable from nearest ticket agent, call on or address,

D. M. KENDRICK, | EDSON J. WEEKS,
Gen. Passenger Agent. | Gen. Agent Pass. Dept.,
Gd. Central Depot, New York. | No. 1, Exchange St., Buffalo.

The Grandest Scenery in America
IS ON THE
NORTH SHORE, LAKE SUPERIOR
—AND—
COLLINGWOOD LINE.
CANADA TRANSIT CO. (LIMITED.)

Steamers leave Collingwood on

TUESDAYS AND FRIDAYS,
On arrival of Morning Trains of the Northern and North-Western Railway from
HAMILTON AND TORONTO.

S.S. CAMPANA, Fast Express Steamer, 1500 tons, Iron, Clyde-built Twin Screw, calls at Meaford, Owen Sound, Bruce Mines, St. Mary' River, Sault, Port Arthur and Duluth direct.

S.S. CITY OF OWEN SOUND, 900 Tons. Meaford, Owen Sound, Killarney, North Channel Ports, Bruce Mines, St. Mary' River, Sault, Michipicoten Island, and around North Shore, Lake Superior, Port Arthur and Duluth.

☞ **Passengers can go by one Steamer and return by the other, thus making complete tour.**

SUMMER EXCURSIONS.

Very low Round Trip Excursion Tickets, all around the Lakes, including Meals and Staterooms.

Through and Return Tickets can be purchased from all Agents Canadian Pacific, Grand Trunk, and Northern and North-Western Railways

JAS. NEIL, Collingwood.
T. MAITLAND, Owen Sound.
R. E. MITCHELL, Port Arthur.
J. T. ROSE, Duluth.

BARLOW CUMBERLAND,
GENERAL AGENT,
85 Yonge St., Toronto

A CONTINUOUS CHAIN OF INTEREST
EXISTS ALONG
The Grand Manitoulin Channel,
THE GREAT NORTHERN TRANSIT CO. (Limited.)

Royal

Mail

Line.

Collingwood

and

Sault Ste.

Marie.

SS Pacific,
Capt. Campbell.

—

SS Atlantic,
Capt. Foote.

—

SS Northern
Belle,
Capt. Barrett.

The new Palace Steamers Pacific and Atlantic leave Collingwood

WEDNESDAYS AND SATURDAYS,

On arrival of morning trains of Northern and North-Western Railways from **Hamilton and Toronto,** calling at Meaford, Owen Sound, Wiarton, thence connecting with Grand Trunk Railway to Killarney, Manitowaning, Little Current, La Cloche, Spanish River, and all the Inner Ports in **The Great North Channel,** St. Joseph's Island, St. Mary's River, Sault Ste. Marie.

☙MACKINAC EXCURSIONS.☙

During the Summer season the Steamers continue their trip round to the far-famed Island of Mackinac, giving sufficient time for Excursionists to visit the many points of beauty and interest.

The cabins are wide, lofty, and every effort used to entertain the Travelling Public with both comfort and hospitality.

PARRY ISLAND ARCHIPELAGO.

S.S. NORTHERN BELLE leaves Collingwood Mondays and Thursdays, 1 p.m., for Parry Sound, passing through all the Islands.

THOS. LONG, Secretary,
COLLINGWOOD.

CHAS. CAMERON, Manager,
COLLINGWOOD.

—THE—
Northern & North-Western Ry

IS THE GREAT AND

ONLY LINE

RUNNING TO THE FAR-FAMED

MUSKOKA DISTRICT,

The Sportsman's Paradise and the
Free Grant Lands of Ontario.

Fast Trains Daily from Toronto and Hamilton, connecting with Steamers of the Muskoka Navigation Company for all Points on the Lakes. Parlour Cars.

Fishing, Hunting, Camping, Delightful Summer Resort for Families, First-Class Hotels at Low Rates.

For a CHEAP TRIP and SOLID COMFORT take the

RELIABLE

Which connects at Collingwood and Penetanguishene with Steamers for Grand and Picturesque Resorts of the Georgian Bay, Lakes Huron and Superior.

TOURISTS' RATES.—Tourists' or Sportsmen's Tickets are good to stop over at any point north of Barrie, and return up till close of Navigation. Camp equipage, stores and dogs are carried free when accompanied by owners.

Baggage checked to principal points on lakes.

For Tickets, Rates, Time Tables, etc., apply to Agents at all principal Ticket Offices in Canada or United States, or to

SAMUEL BARKER,
Gen. Manager, Toronto.

BARLOW CUMBERLAND,
Ticket Agent, 35 Yonge St., Toronto.

ROBERT QUINN,
Gen. Pass. Agent, Toronto.

MUSKOKA & NIPISSING NAV. CO.

DAILY PASSENGER STEAMERS

Upon the Lakes of Muskoka, between Gravenhurst, (on the N. & N.W. Railway), Bracebridge, Beaumaris, Bala, Port Carling, Windermere, Port Sandfield, Rosseau and Port Cookburn, &c.

Upon the Upper Maganetawan Waters, between Buck's Falls on the N. & P.J. Railway), Maganetewan Village, Depot Farms and Ah-Mic Harbour.

Upon Lake Nipissing, between North Bay, (upon the C. P. Railway), Callander, Nipissing Village, &c.

The Most Attractive and Popular Resorts in America.

EXCURSION TICKETS,

Good for THIRTY or more days, to be had in the principal cities and towns of Canada and the United States.

SPECIAL STEAMERS, NICELY FITTED UP FOR THE USE OF PRIVATE PARTIES,

To be had at moderate rates.

Good Hotel accommodation abounds throughout the Lake Districts at moderate rates.

ROBT. QUINN,
Gen. Pass. Agent
N. & N. W. Railways.

A. P. COCKBURN,
Gen. Manager
M. & N. Nav. Co'y.

TORONTO TICKET AGENCY at B. CUMBERLAND'S, 35 Yonge St.

HUDSON RIVER BY DAYLIGHT
—VIA THE—
DAY LINE
Of Palace Steamers on the Hudson River
—AND THE—
New York Central & Hudson River R.R.

Leave Albany 8.30 a.m., Arrive at New York 5.30 p.m

Leave New York (Sunday excepted), Vestry St. Pier, 8.40 a.m 22nd St. Pier, N. R., 9 a.m., (making principal landings) arriving Albany (foot Hamilton St.). 6.10 p.m.

Trains from Utica, Geneva, Niagara Falls, Buffalo, Lewiston, Toronto, Cleveland, Chicago, Alexandria Bay and the Thousand Islands, reach ALBANY in t to connect with the Morning Boat for New York, and going North Trains leave after arriva Boat. Berths in Sleeping Cars can be secured on the Steamer.

Be Sure and Secure Tickets via this Route.

Dining Rooms on main deck, *a la carte*, open from 7 a.m. Drawing Rooms for Parties.

C. T. VAN SANTVOORD, VESTRY STREET PIER, C. R. VANBENTHUYS
Gen'l Manager.   New York City.   Gen'l Ticket Agent.

PEOPLE'S LINE

NEW YORK TO ALBANY.

DREW, - Capt. S. J. Roe. | ST. JOHN, Capt. Thos. Po

FROM PIER 41, NORTH RIVER,

South Side of Canal Street, near Jersey City Ferry, Debrosses Street,

AT 6.00 P.M.

Connecting at Albany, except Sunday, with trains of the New York Central for the West, with trains for Saratoga and all the summer resorts of Lake George and Lake Champlain.

ALBANY TO NEW YORK.

ST. JOHN, Capt. Thos. Post. | DREW, - Capt. S. J. R

LEAVE ALBANY AT 8.00 P.M.

On arrival of trains from the NORTH and WEST, change from cars to Boat.

Baggage transferred FREE between N. Y. Central R.R. and Steamers at Alba

TICKETS and STATEROOMS secured by telegraph and telephone in Albany, at the Off Steamboat Square, and tickets for sale at all the principal railroad ticket offices in the EA NORTH and SOUTH.

J. H. ALLAIRE, Gen. Ticket Agent.   M. B. WATERS, Gen. Pass. Agent.
E. C. SHAFFER, Agent, Albany.

Summit House and Island Park,
Port Cockburn, Lake Joseph, Muskoka.
— FOR —
FAMILIES, TOURISTS AND SPORTSMEN.

This favourite house has been enlarged this season, making it the largest hotel in Muskoka; is beautifully situated at the head of Lake Joseph (the prettiest of the Muskoka Lakes); commands fine lake and forest views; daily steamer, post and telegraph offices in house.

EXCELLENT BLACK AND ROCK BASS, PICKEREL AND SALMON TROUT FISHING.

HAMILTON FRASER, - Proprietor.

LAKES OF MUSKOKA.
Boats, Yachts, Canoes, Tents for Hire.

TOURISTS AND CAMPING PARTIES
Supplied at Moderate Rates.

Boats Forwarded to any Point Desired.

A Good supply is kept by the undersigned at Port Carling and Windermere as well as Rosseau, where all applications should be sent.

OARS, PADDLES AND ROWLOCKS KEPT FOR SALE.

HENRY DITCHBURN,
Boat Builder, Rosseau

MAPLEHURST
Summer Hotel,
LAKE ROSSEAU.

This hotel has just been erected regardless of expense, with a view to the comfort of the summer tourists, and is charmingly situated on one of the most romantic spots on these waters. A first class table will be kept and every possible amusement for the guests. A daily mail will be brought to the house and constant communication kept by ferry with Rosseau, which is three-quarters of a mile distant. The steamboat calls daily, leaving guests right at their destination. A fleet of boats will be kept at the house, which is surrounded by a charming grove of silver birch, ashen, and evergreen.

PARTIES WHO DESIRE TO SPEND A PLEASANT SUMMER WITH PLENTY OF

BOATING, FISHING, BATHING

Etc, will find this resort one of the most comfortable and commodious on this beautiful of air of lakes.

J. P. BROWN, Propr.

1869. ESTABLISHED 1869.

SEWELL BROS.,
Grocers and Italian Warehousemen,
IMPORTERS OF

Fine Wines, English and French Fancy Groceries

AND DEALERS IN ALL KINDS OF

TOURISTS' SUPPLIES,
No. 32 JAMES ST.,

HAMILTON, CANADA.

Intending Tourists and Camping Parties to our Northern Lakes and other parts of Western Canada, during the coming summer will find it to their advantage to purchase their supplies from us.

Send for catalogue and prices.

All orders by mail will receive prompt and careful attention.

Merchants Line.

MONTREAL, TORONTO, CLEVELAND, CHICAGO.

UPPER CABIN STEAMERS

Armenia, Cuba and California.

These Steamers have magnificent full length cabins, and are elegantly fitted up, and have all the comforts and conveniences of a first-class hotel. State-rooms are all furnished with woven wire mattresses, making the most luxuriously comfortable bed. They will ply regularly between MONTREAL & CHICAGO calling at all principal way-ports, during the season of navigation, passing through the beautiful Scenery of the Thousand Islands, calling at TORONTO every THURSDAY at 10 a.m., going east, and 9.30 p.m., going west. Berths can be secured in advance by applying to

HAGARTY & CO.,
56 King St. East, Toronto.

Or to

B. CUMBERLAND,
35 Yonge St., Toronto.

LAKE ROSSEAU.

THE NEW HOTEL
At the Head of the Lake and near the Shadow River.

MAPLEHURST—LAKE ROSSEAU.

Special Rates Made for Families.   Correspondence Solic

J. P. BROWN, Proprie^or.

MUSKOKA LAKES.

Prospect House Hotel,

PORT SANDFIELD,

ENOCH COX, Proprietor.

Terms, $1.50 Per Day. Special Terms for Families.

The Hotel stands at the junction of LAKES ROSSEAU and JOSEPH, commands a fine view of both lakes; can accommodate over one hundred guests; roomy piazzas extend around the house. An excellent table is also set at this house and is one of its leading features, and no pains will be spared by the proprietor to make the stay of guests at Prospect House pleasant in every respect.

Gentlemen visiting the Lakes, accompanied by their families, will find Prospect House a very desirable house to stay at.

Ladies and young people can here indulge in boating without the least danger, as it is always free from rough water.

A FINE SANDY BEACH FOR BATHING.

It is well noted for its

Pickerel and Bass Fishing.

The steam yacht "Sunbeam" makes daily trips from the Hotel during the entire season. Post-office on the premises; daily mail.

PROSPECT HOUSE, in the fall, is a favourite resort for sportsmen. Guides and hounds kept.

Port Carling Summer Retreat
CHERRY GROVE.
VANDERBURGH HOUSE.

Tourists will not find flies here at any season of the year, making a ver desirable place in the early part of Summer for Tourists wishing to spend the most desirable part of the season in pure air.

THE PICTURESQUE STEAM LAUNCH

"KATE MURRAY."

A great favourite with American and Canadian tourists is owned by tl Proprietor of the House; the "Kate" has been refitted with new engine and is the fastest Yacht on these Lakes, and may be hired on reasonab terms to touch at all points of interest.

---o---

Building Material delivered to any part of Lake by Contract. Address communications to
C. W. VANDERBURGH.

STRATTON HOUSE
PORT CARLING.

This Hotel is delightfully situated at the junction of Indian River ar Lake Rosseau. Passengers from Toronto and Hamilton arrive here from 4 to 5 p.m. the same day.

A very convenient stopping place. Guests patronizing the house w find it as comfortable as any Hotel on the Lakes, and their wan promptly attended to.

Accommodation for 50 people. The rooms are large and airy, and liberal table is a leading feature of the House. The surrounding scene being fine, artists will find full scope for their pencils. Sportsmen w have some of the best bass fishing to be had on these waters, as Lal Rosseau and Muskoka, as well as Silver Lake are within very ea distance of the House.

A commodious enclosed Bathing House for Visitors. Lawn Tenr Ground. A superior class of Boats on hand for hire by the day or wee

Terms for Board, from $1.25 per day.—Special terms by the week or month.

JOHN FRASER, Proprieto

Monteith House,
ROSSEAU.

Good Accommodation for Tourists.

FIRST-CLASS TABLE,
LARGE ROOMS,
BATH ROOMS, &c.

Billard Room and Roller Skating Rink.

JOHN MONTEITH, Propr.

Craigielea House,
LAKE JOSEPH.

This house has been improved and refitted since last season and visitors will find comfortable quarters and some of the

Best Fishing in the District.

Close to the entrance to Little Lake Joseph.

JOHN C. WALLS,
Proprietor.

PORT CARLING

POST-OFFICE STORE

—FULL SUPPLY OF—

Dry Goods, Boots & Shoes, Hardware

FRESH GROCERIES AND PROVISIONS.

CAMPING PARTIES AND TOURISTS WILL FIND Fishing Tackle, Butter, Eggs, Fresh Bread always on hand.

PROMPT ATTENTION GIVEN TO BUSINESS.

W. HANNA & CO.

CAMPERS, TOURISTS, SPORTSMEN
—GO TO—
JORDAN'S
General Store,
ROSSEAU,

FOR

Fishing Tackle, Tents, Coal Oil Stoves

AND ALL SUPPLIES.

TENTS FOR HIRE.

—NEW—

SAW and PLANING MILL.

The undersigned has erected a new saw and planing mill near Craigielea, at the entrance to Little Lake Joseph, where he will keep a supply of all kinds of rough and dressed

LUMBER AND SHINGES.

Building Contracts Taken

ESTIMATES FURNISHED.

THOMAS WATERS,
Craigielea P.O., Lake Joseph.

AH-MIC HARBOUR,

One of the best locations for Sportsmen and tourists in Parry Sound District; can reach it from Toronto the same day by Gravenhurst and Burk's Falls, down the Maganetewan River into Ah-Mic Lake; good accommodation for travellers or tourists; the best **Hunting** and **Fishing** in the district; boats and livery on hand; charges moderate; mail three times a week; steamboat lands at the door; goat's milk kept for sickly children and adults, which is highly recommended.

JOHN CROSWELL, PROP'R,
Ah-Mic Harbour, P.O., Muskoka.

PORT CARLING.

—GO TO—

JOS. S. WALLIS'

General Merchant

FOR

Dry Goods, Groceries, Boots & Shoes,

HARDWARE,

Lumber, Timber and Shingles.

PLANING AND MATCHING A SPECIALTY.

BUILDERS' SUPPLIES.

Communications by letter promptly answered.

PORT CARLING.

CAMPERS AND TOURISTS'
SUPPLIES.

DEALER IN GOOD FRESH

GROCERIES
—AND—
PROVISIONS,
CONFECTIONERY,
FISHING TACKLE.
—ALSO—
DRY GOODS
—AND—
BOOTS & SHOES.

Canned Goods of Every Description.

FREDERICK D. STUBBS,

OAKLAND PARK HOTEL,

Opposite Head of Port Carling River, Lake Rosseau.

———o———

This new Hotel commands extensive views over the greater portion of Lake Rosseau, both east and west, including Windermere.

Good Bathing. Steamboat Wharf. Boats can be had on application.

Terms from $1.25 per day. Special Rates to Families.

JOSEPH M. TOBIN, - - Proprietor,

PORT CARLING

THE
BELVIDERE HOTEL
PARRY SOUND.

This Hotel is open during the Summer Season to re ceive guests. The Hotel occupies a beautiful and com manding position on a height of land overlooking th waters and numerous islands of Parry Sound. The a is pure and the scenery beautiful. The numerous is lands and channels are very picturesque and affor excellent opportunities for boating, camping and fishin

RICHARD GODOLPHIN,
Land and Estate Agent, Auctioneer, Conveyance

COMMISSIONER FOR TAKING AFFIDAVITS IN H. C. J.

HUNTSVILLE, - - - - ONTARIO.

FERNDALE HOUSE,

LAKE ROSSEAU,

NEAR PORT CARLING.

R. G. PENSON, - PROPRIETOR.

Picturesquely Situated.

Good Fishing, Boats, etc., etc.

Daily Mail. Steamboat Calls.

TERMS VERY MODERATE.

FOR PARTICULARS APPLY TO

R. G. PENSON, PORT CARLING.

CLEVELAND'S
LAKE ROSSEAU,
MUSKOKA.

Parties visiting Muskoka will find this a most pleasant and comfortable summer resort. Every attention paid to the comfort of guests. Good Bathing and Fishing. Daily Steamboat.

GOOD TABLE.

C. J. MINETT.

BOATS AT REASONABLE RATES.

HUNTSVILLE.

DOMINION HOTEL.

Tourists and the Travelling Public entertained in a manner unequalled outside Toronto.

Fishing and Shooting.

Table and Wines first-rate. Good Stabling accommodation. Five minutes' walk from Railway Depot of Northern and Pacific Junction.
Terms Moderate.

JAMES W. JACOBS, - - **Proprietor.**

LAKE MUSKOKA.

BEAUMARIS HOTEL

Tondern Island.

Good Fishing, Boating and Bathing;

Billiard Room, Bowling Alley;

Lawn Tennis and Croquet Ground

BOATS AND GUIDES FOR HIRE.

Board $1.50 to $2.00 Per Day.

SPECIAL RATES MADE WITH FAMILIES

Business men joining their families by the Saturday expres trains arrive at Beaumaris early Saturday afternoon, before tea time, and do not leave until after usual breakfast on Monday morning, giving ample time for a pleasant rest.

Daily Mail.

EDWARD PROWSE, Proprietor.

LAKE ROSSEAU.

WINDERMERE HOUSE,

Situated on the Shores of

LAKE ROSSEAU, MUSKOKA.

Improvements constantly being made with the view of adding to the comfort and pleasure of its guests. For description of surroundings, see page 121 of Guide.

TERMS:—from $1.25 to $1.50 PER DAY.

SPECIAL RATES TO FAMILIES.

THOMAS AITKEN, - Proprietor.

BAYSVILLE.

FOREST HOUSE,

JORDAN KEELER, Proprietor.

Tourists can enjoy unrivalled scenery on "Lake of Bays." Two first-class steamboats ply on its waters during season; rare sport for Speckled Trout in this region; the neighbouring woods abound in Deer and Partridge; ample accommodation; an excellent table; every attention to guests.

THE NORTHERN,

(ERECTED 1884.)

Port Arthur, Canada.

THE FINEST HOTEL IN WESTERN CANADA.

The Canadian Pacific Trains east and west stop here 30 minutes for dinner.

F. S. WILEY, MANAGER.

GLOBE HOTEL

COLLINGWOOD, ONT.
TERMS—1.50 PER DAY.

This Hotel commands a fine view of the Collingwood Harl and Mountain, rendering it a pleasant resort to Tourists, to whom the best of attention is paid.

Free 'Bus to and from all Trains and Bo(Telephone Communication with all parts the town.

JOHN ROWLAND,
Proprietc

CENTRAL HOTEI
COLLINGWOOD, ONT.

Telephone Communication with all parts of the town.

THOMAS COLLINS,   ··   -   Proprie

PAUL'S HOTEL,
MEAFORD.

TERMS, $1.50 per day.
Special Rates for Families. Pleasant Verandahs and Gardens on the River Bank.

FREE 'BUS TO ALL TRAINS & BOATS.

MRS. S. PAUL.

NOBLE'S HOTEL,
MEAFORD, ONT.
RATES, $1.00 per day.
SPECIAL RATES given for Families by the Week.

—:o:—

Boats can be hired at reasonable Rates.
PLENTY OF FRESH FISH AND FRESH AIR.
—:o:—
JUST THE PLACE TO SPEND A QUIET HOLIDAY.

JAMES NOBLE,
PROPRIETOR.

FISHING TACKL[E]

Rods,   F[
Lines,   Needle[s
Flies,   and
Hooks,
Baits,   Small[

TORONTO WAREHOUSE.

ALLCOCK, LAIGHT & WESTWO[OD]
MANUFACTURERS,
REDDITCH, ENGLAND, and
6 Wellington Street West, Toronto, Onta[rio]

B. WESTWOOD,
Resident Partner.

N. B.—[
Rods &[
made on [pre]mises.

AMERICAN HOTEL

COR. YONGE and FRONT STS., TORONTO, ONT.

ED. H. EDSALL, Manager.　　　　　THOS. TAYLOR, Propr.
H. G. EDSALL, Clerk.

RATES, $2.00 PER DAY

And graded according to rooms.

SPECIAL RATES TO THEATRICAL PEOPLE AND THE COMMERCIAL TRADE.

This favourite old hostelier has just undergone a thorough course of renovating, remodeling and refitting throughout, and now stands second to no $2.00 per day house in the Dominion. The *cuisine* will be found equal to that of any hotel in the Queen City, and neither pains nor expense are spared in seeing that guests are properly cared for.

The AMERICAN is the only hotel in Toronto running FREE 'BUSS to and from all trains, steamboats, etc., and it is safe to say that guests once stopping there will not fail to do so again.

REVERE HOUSE,

COR. KING AND YORK STREETS,

TORONTO.

Situated in the business portion of the City.

Five minutes walk from the Union Depot.

Street Cars pass the door to all parts.

THE BEST $1.50 Per Day HOUSE IN CANADA.

SPECIAL ATTENTION TO TOURISTS.

J. J. JAMESON,　　-　　-　　Proprietor.

www.ingramcontent.com/pod-product-compliance
Lightning Source LLC
Chambersburg PA
CBHW031347230426
43670CB00006B/459